D0838316

Robert P. Odenwald, M.D.

YOUR CHILD'S WORLD

FROM INFANCY THROUGH ADOLESCENCE

IMAGE BOOKS

A Division of Doubleday & Company, Inc.
Garden City, New York

Image Books Edition 1963
by special arrangement with Random House, Inc.

Image Books edition published September 1963

Nihil obstat: FRANCIS J. CONNELL, C. SS. R., S. T. D.
　　　　　　　Censor Deputatus
Imprimatur: PATRICK A. O'BOYLE
　　　　　　　Archbishop of Washington
　　　　　　　July 10, 1958

Contents

CHAPTER ONE   Your Child's Basic Needs   11

The Basic Factors That Form Your Child's Personality. How Heredity Deals the Cards But Environment Plays the Hand. Helping Your Child Meet His First Challenge of Life. How To Foster a Feeling of Security by Giving Uniform, Sympathetic Care. Types of Parents Who Reject Their Children. The Twin Evils of Perfectionism and Overprotectiveness. Your Child Needs Freedom To Develop. Teaching Your Child To Do Things for Himself. Why You Should Avoid Physical and Emotional Restraints. Your Child's Need To Feel Competent. Giving Your Child a Sense of Adequacy.

CHAPTER TWO   Your Child from Birth to Two   23

Early Feeding Problems. Sucking—the Baby's First Psychological Pleasure. The New Trend to Breast Feeding. Toilet Training—How Psychiatrists View the Problem. General Principles To Follow. Undesirable Results of Improper Training. Relationship Between Toilet Training and Sex Attitudes. How To Regard Your Child's Genital Play. A Baby's Primitive Pleasures—Movement for Its Own Sake. "The Need to Grab Things." Your Infant—Source of Your Happiness.

CHAPTER THREE   From Baby to Child—Ages Three to
                                              Five   33

The "Exploring Stage." Learning by Seeing, Hearing, Tasting, and Touching. The Increase of Daring as Your Child's World Expands. "Destructiveness"—a Form of Creativeness. The Thumb-Sucking Problem. The "Demanding Stage." Techniques Your Child Uses To Command Attention. Bed Wetting—Its Physical and Emotional Causes. Possessiveness and Your Child's Discovery That He Can Protect His Property Verbally. Boastfulness, Quarrelsomeness, and Negativism. Symptoms of Jealousy in Your Child. The Nursery

School Stage. Learning To Live with Others. Fears, Temper Tantrums, and Vivid Imaginings—Signs of Adjustment. How To Handle Children's Lies.

CHAPTER FOUR   Your Child Becomes an Individual   53

Your Child's Desire To Be Recognized as a "Person," and To Prove His Growing Powers. Factors That Threaten a Child's Sense of Belonging. Self-Expression Comes to the Fore—An Inner Drive for Independence. Fashioning of the Superego. How the Id, Ego, and Superego Affect the Development of Personality. Different Stages of Personality Development Determine How You Should Discipline Your Child. Punishment Should Fit the Offense and Must Be Consistent. Other Rules of Discipline. Teaching Your Child To Accept Life's Disappointments. How Inability To Handle Frustrations Can Mar the Personality. The "Normal" Fears of Childhood. Nightmares—a Disguised Fear of Physical Punishment. How To Make Your Child Less Fearful. How To Handle Sex Problems at This Stage. Factors in Masturbation and Other Sex Experiences. Training in Self-Control—Necessary for Effective Sex Instruction.

CHAPTER FIVE   The Personality of Preadolescents—
                              Ages Six to Eleven   76

The "Golden Age" of Childhood. How To Develop Your Child's Conscience. Different Behavioral Patterns for Boys and Girls. Separate "Must-Nots" and "Must-Dos" for the Sexes. Social Laws and Taboos—Differences Between Upper and Lower Class Environments. Opportunities for Parents To Provide Affectionate Guidance. Your Child's Developing Aptitudes and Interests. How Some Mothers Smother Children with Love. The Abnormality of Absolute Cleanliness in Children. The Father's Responsibility To Give a Child Security. A Boy's Identification with the Dominant Parent and His Need for "Hero" Worship. How the School Can Influence Personality. How Parents Can Make Up for Defects of Teachers. Truancy—Last Resort of the Unhappy Child. Playmates, Playthings, and Their Effect upon Personality. How Firm Religious Beliefs Serve Your Child in Adolescence and Adulthood.

CHAPTER SIX   Personality Adjustment of Adolescence   101

No Longer Child, Not Yet an Adult. How the Increasing Gland Activity Affects Your Youngster's Personality. Primary Sex Changes at Puberty. How To Explain the "Coming of Age" to Your Children. Boys Who Are Too Short and Girls Who Are Too Tall. Learning to Accept Responsibilities of Adulthood. Psychological Changes of Adolescence. The Normality of Your Child's Struggle for Independence. Every Teen-Ager Needs a Pal. Areas of Common Conflict Between Parent and Adolescent. Tips on Allowances for Teen-Agers. Emotional Excesses of Adolescents—Should They Be Ignored or Rebuked? Standards—Usually Set by the Group.

CHAPTER SEVEN   Adolescent "Stress and Storm"   123

Moral Values of the Adolescent. Individual Differences. Teen-Age Delinquency. Types of Adolescent Offenses. Sex Awareness—Its Problems. Sexual Perversion.

CHAPTER EIGHT   The Maladjusted Child   161

Physical Handicaps. Psychosomatic Illnesses. Social Maladjustments. Maladjusted Children from Broken Homes. Neglect and Overprotection—How Extremes of Parental Conduct Cause Maladjustments. Problem Children from Rich Homes. Dangers to Personality Development When a Child Cannot Keep Pace in School.

CHAPTER NINE   How Psychiatry Helps the Maladjusted   181

Types of Children Who Need Psychiatric Care. Importance of Detecting Symptoms Early. Limitations of Psychiatric Treatment. Different Kinds of Treatment. Physical Methods—Water Baths, Surgery, Drugs. Mental Methods—Interviews, Analysis, Play Therapy. How a Psychiatrist Treats a Typical Child Patient. How Child Guidance Clinics Work. What Play Therapy Reveals About a Patient.

YOUR CHILD'S WORLD

CHAPTER ONE

Your Child's Basic Needs

Your Child Needs Security

As a parent, you will greatly influence the development of your child's personality. You can help him achieve attitudes and outlooks that will enable him to reach adulthood as a mature, well-adjusted individual. To a large extent, how you use your power will determine what kind of person your child will be.

Your power is limited, however; for you had no control over the basic factors that went into the making of your child's personality. These were determined at the marvelous moment of conception. At that precise instant when the male sperm fused with the female ovum to create a new human life, much of your child's physical endowment—his general physique, the color of his skin, hair and eyes, his intellectual capacity, his muscular tonus, his emotional excitability—was determined. The basic ingredients in your child's personality are fashioned by heredity as it is miraculously compressed into the tiny fertilized egg in the womb.

These basic traits of personality can be *changed* only by accident, disease, age, or surgery. But they can be *tuned up* or *toned down* by parental training and life experience and by his own deliberate self-control of these factors. As has been said often, heredity deals the cards but environment plays them in the game: your child's personality will develop as his God-given traits are molded by family, school, and church training, by ever changing environmental factors, by national and racial characteristics and trends, by friendships, by social pressures—in fact, by every experience of living.

Thus, your child's eventual personality results from the interplay between his native endowment and environmental influences, and by the exertion of his own will.

No two children, nor two adults, are exactly the same. Each has his own personality: his own distinctive physical and mental qualities, his own habits of behavior. I have seen identical twins reared in the same environment, equally loved and treated alike as nearly as possible. They can hardly be distinguished from each other physically, yet always can be recognized by their different responses. Not all their experiences have been alike, and since experiences play an integral part in the personality, their reactions—especially their emotional responses—often differ.

The development of your child's native traits into his personality begins soon after birth, when he begins crying for nourishment and attention, cooing when his wishes are satisfied, screaming when he is denied or unattended. He develops habits of reacting to various influences.

During his preschool years, he learns other patterns of behavior. For example, he learns to conform to certain rules; otherwise he will be punished either by loss of love or spanking. At nursery school he learns that there are further laws of conduct which apply not only to himself but to all the other children in the group. He takes his first step in social conformity, and lessons he learns in conducting himself with other individuals may well influence his relations with other persons throughout his life. It may not be too far-fetched to say that the executive of a large corporation, whose success lies in getting along with people, learned how to do it on a sand pile.

As we all know, life is a process of continual change. And how all of us adjust to change—from the effortless existence inside the womb to the life following birth, from infancy to childhood, from childhood to adolescence, from adolescence to maturity, and from maturity to old age—determines how well we develop and how happy we are. Such changes may make us more self-reliant, better adjusted, more confident of our ability to face the realities of life, or they may leave deep psychological wounds, which may return to plague us at every further stage of our existence.

Consider, for example, the abrupt and extensive changes that take place even in normal birth. Before your child was born, he led a peaceful, protected existence. All his wants were satisfied. From his mother's body he received food, shelter, and warmth. When at birth he is abruptly separated from the all-satisfying warmth and protection of his mother's womb, for the first time, his security is disrupted. This change is the greatest your child will ever know and requires the greatest adjustment he will ever make.

How we help the baby meet his first challenge of life will have an effect upon his personality. If we push him into a corner of a room, hold a bottle to his mouth every four hours on schedule, and never hold him in our arms, we should not be surprised if he becomes nervous, irritable, and neurotic.

An infant's loss of protection should be compensated for by a new source of support. So a new security is given the infant: he is made to feel that he is still part of his mother's body by being sheltered in her arms, by the soft pressure of her caresses, and by nestling at her breast while satisfying his hunger.

The loving protection which a mother gives her new-born child may be considered almost instinctive. It is found in the most primitive societies. But when we first adopted the practice of having babies in hospitals and developed satisfactory formulas for feeding them, we lost sight of the importance of providing a continuity of security from the periods before and after birth. Hospitals isolated the infant from his mother except at feeding time. Babies lost that essential feeling of security—and their insecurity sometimes remained with them all their lives. Today, we try to concentrate on welcoming the new-born child into his new environment and making him feel at home. Some hospitals keep the infant in the same room with the mother, encourage her to hold him in her arms, and allow the father to visit the mother and baby together.

Your first responsibility as a parent—to give your child a sense of security—is one which will continue throughout his growing-up process. His need for security—and your obligation to provide it—will be the most important part of your relationship with him. His behavior in later life will reflect whether you have provided or denied it. Many of his actions which you may regard as behavioral problems may be his way of expressing his need for it. How successful he becomes as a mature individual will depend greatly upon how much of it you have given him in his infancy and childhood.

You can best foster a feeling of security in your infant or young child by giving him uniform, sympathetic care. Paying loving attention to his needs, like holding him, rocking him, creates a steadfast continuity, which makes him feel secure. One of the first things you will discover about your child is his urgent demand for consistency. Take him from the crib to which he has become accustomed, change some characteristic of his feedings, misplace his favorite toy, get someone new to care for him for a short period, and he may wail for hours. Is this an early evidence of perverseness on his part? No. It is evidence of his desire for security and his deep unhappiness when it is not provided for him.

You will also soon learn that security for any youngster comes, to a great extent, from learning to do things for himself rather than from depending upon you. Therefore, as your child grows, you should constantly stimulate him to fulfill his own wants. If he drops his toy from his play pen and learns to reach through the bars to retrieve it, he is making a better adjustment to reality—and therefore has a greater feeling of security—than the youngster who depends upon his parents to do things he could well do for himself.

Your Child Needs To Be Wanted

One of the serious threats to a youngster's security is the feeling that his parents do not truly want or love him. This feeling of rejection can be caused by many factors and can be expressed in many different ways. It can create serious psychological disturbances in the child. Some parents who reject their child would vehemently deny that they do so. They may not be even remotely aware of what they are doing; they may consider themselves to be the most conscientious of parents. Unfortunately, deep in their unconscious, they may have reasons for not wanting the child and may subconsciously cover up these reasons by attempting to be overly attentive.

Some couples resent having a child because he interferes with their pleasurable way of life. For example, many young married couples are unwilling to deny themselves the parties, dances, sports, and other amusements which they would be forced to curtail in order to care for a child. Others do not want to make economic sacrifices, which they feel having children will require. Many young wives, with their husband's willing consent, work to provide luxuries, which they would need to forego if they had children. Other young wives continue to work to keep their financial, psychological, and social independence: they believe that having children would make them dependent upon their husbands, and this condition, in their view, would be a fatal handicap in their struggle for equality.

Some couples are so immature that they dread the responsibility of parenthood: to them, the coming of a baby is a calamity. Some couples are unable to get along: in this case, either or both parties may reject the baby because he is regarded as a chain which binds them to the unhappy home situation.

This rejection of the child usually takes one of several principal forms. The obvious form—overt rejection—is fortunately the most infrequent. In fact, we are deeply shocked whenever we encounter evidences of it: for example, a mother may deposit her child on a doorstep and disappear; a man may desert his wife and thrust upon her the complete responsibility for the care and upbringing of the children; a mother may announce openly that she hates her child, treat him in a noticeably hostile manner, and be completely indifferent to his basic needs and natural desires.

Parents who practice overt rejection at least operate in an uncomplicated fashion. But motives are not so simple to detect when dealing with the more conventional rejection—that of the perfectionistic parents—which takes a concealed form.

Perfectionistic parents are usually secret rejectors of their children. I recall parents in a well-to-do section who were extremely rigid in dealing with their two youngsters. The little boy and girl were required to rise each morning at an early hour, practice musical instruments for half an hour before breakfast, and leave at a specific moment for school every day. They had their entire leisure time carefully scheduled like a railroad train. The parents insisted that the letter of their law be followed to the last iota. They insisted that the children always have clean faces, hands, shoes and clothing and never, under pain of severe punishment, must they do anything that might reflect upon their parents. The mother and father argued long and loudly that they were good parents and were merely establishing order and discipline in their children's lives. But a careful study of their background revealed that actually they did not want children because they believed the children would interfere with their professional and social ambitions. Of course, "nice" people do not openly reject their children; thus, in this instance, true feelings found an outlet in a disguised form.

It is unnatural and impossible for children to entirely comply with the demands of perfectionistic adults. Indeed, not even other adults can live satisfactorily with a perfectionist.

Demands that your child be properly groomed at all times and that the house be always spotless make him feel insecure with his position because of his helplessness in the face of such strictness. The perfectionistic parent can never be satisfied, because no child can be perfect, however hard he tries.

The child who is openly rejected may express his insecurity by acting hostile and aggressive. The child who receives the perfectionist's rejection, on the other hand, is more likely to exhibit feelings of inferiority, discouragement, and depression.

Another form of rejection may sound like a contradiction of terms. This is a rejection which is manifested in an overprotective attitude. We all know of the overprotective mother: she cannot let her child out of her sight for an instant for fear that he may injure himself. When her eight-year-old boy wants to run, as normal boys do, she orders him to stop for fear that he may fall and hurt himself. When her teenage daughter wants to take a shopping trip, the mother must go along for fear that her daughter may get lost or make a poor purchase. She won't let her boy engage in sports—they are too rough—and if he seems to be faring poorly at school, she appears at the principal's office to see what is wrong, not with her youngster, but with the teacher.

This overprotective attitude results from what we term psychological overcompensation. In such cases, parents are really rejecting their child, but due to certain moral or social forces, they feel guilty about this conscious attitude. Consequently, they push their true feeling down into their unconscious and, to placate their sense of guilt, smother the youngster with love and attention.

Here is a typical example of overprotection. A young mother of three small children is deserted by her husband. She wants to lead a life of freedom but instead she must work to support them and be both father and mother to them. She prepares their breakfast and sends them off to school, comes home to get their lunch and, after her day's work, prepares the dinner and does the housework. During week ends she shops, mends, and keeps an anxious eye on the children. Whenever she can, she lavishes love upon her little ones and worries constantly about their safety. Overprotected, they have developed no self-dependency or responsibility. They cannot go to their bedroom without her, nor go to sleep without her final kiss. They continually battle for her favor and embraces. She never takes a trip without them and worries until she gets them safely home again.

Children of such parents are apt to be completely spoiled. They are given everything they desire, even things beyond the parents' means. They are protected from all harm and evil. Their health and physical safety are a constant worry to the parent. Their activities are closely supervised so that they cannot hurt themselves. They cannot enter actively into any sport; they must not play with rough children; they cannot go on trips alone. Their activities, in fact their very lives, are restricted by their seemingly doting parents. Again we find a paradoxical situation. The parents would never dream of actually killing their child, yet overprotected children are psychologically "killed with love."

Overprotected children are often prevented from reaching maturity, from becoming independent adults: they rarely acquire self-confidence, or learn to accept responsibility and are often rejected by their fellow men, because although they have reached the age of manhood or womanhood, they have not emotionally matured.

If parents seem oversolicitous for their child, we are not free to deduce that rejection is necessarily at the root of this devotion. There may be other reasons for the parents' defending attitude. Parents who have had only one child, perhaps late in their married life, may be extremely careful about him. Parents who have lost a child by death may overprotect the remaining one. A child who has endured long illness—such as one with heart disease following rheumatic fever—may continue to be treated as a chronic invalid. Such treatment, while often not desirable, may not be due to any lack of love on the parents' part.

Your Child Needs Freedom To Develop

Since the young child develops a sense of security through the use and development of his own abilities, it is advisable not to try to restrain him physically. Even in this generation, some parents tie the baby's hands to prevent thumb sucking, or tie his arms so that he will not pull the blankets over his head and perhaps suffocate. Frequently the baby is physically restrained by being left in bed too long, by being left in one position too long, or by being left in a bed that is too small, too soft, or both. Some parents securely bind the hands and legs of the child so that only a minimum of movement is possible. All of these restraining practices are wrong. They deny him the reasonable opportunity to kick and wriggle about freely, to develop his muscles and, most important, to learn the capabilities of his organs.

Too much physical restriction of your child may produce one or two psychological effects: he may become hyperactive, tense, and nervous; or, he may develop a strong and lasting antagonism toward restraints of either a physical or psychological type.

There is another type of restraint that can also mar his personality—the moral restraint which prevents him from enjoying the normal activities of childhood. Do you find yourself saying no to your youngster without thinking? Do you prevent him from developing his normal curiosity about things and places around him? Do you find his infantile babblings and attempt at speech too bothersome to understand? If you do, there is a danger that you may weaken his respect for you, and ultimately for all authority.

Some youngsters develop such a determination to attack the bonds of authority and to eliminate restraint that it becomes an actual obsession in their adult life. For example, I know of one boy who grew up hearing from morning to night that he couldn't do this and mustn't do that. Whenever he persisted in doing what he was told not to do, he was quickly and thoroughly punished. Johnny saw other youngsters doing things that were forbidden him, and their parents didn't seem to mind. So it was not long before he became defiant of all authority. He would climb to high swaying branches of trees and watch with ill-concealed delight the fear written on his mother's face below. Johnny was expressing his resentment of the fact that the excessive discipline to which he was exposed was meted out without any compensating display of affection.

I had the opportunity to observe Johnny as he developed into adolescence and adulthood. Breaking rules seemed to become his major delight. He was repeatedly in trouble. He was expelled from private schools and military academies. In the Army, he achieved a series of promotions; but then his deep-seated rebellion against authority asserted itself anew, and he was reduced to private. After the war, he began moving from job to job. Eventually, each employer would ask him to do things he did not want to do. Rebellion against authority by now was Johnny's second nature, so he rebelled—and soon was seeking another job.

Of course, it is a long road from childhood insecurity to the inability to hold a job in later life. But the relationship is very plain to those who have the opportunity of observing how overstrict and unloving parental discipline can affect a child's sense of security and cause him to react in a hostile way.

It may be useful to summarize what we have discussed thus far: Above all else, your child needs security. He needs your love and affection. He will achieve a sense of security if he is permitted to grow as an independent individual.

Let us now examine how these principles are related to conditions you will encounter as your child grows.

When he is an infant—until he reaches the age of three— he is content to be a baby. He makes few demands other than those necessary to satisfy his basic physical needs and his fundamental needs for security. He emerges from babyhood into childhood at approximately four. Now he has additional demands which he will continue to make for the rest of his life. Now his sense of security depends not only on his parents' love, but also upon his own sense of adequacy as an individual.

Security is the most important asset of personality because in order to achieve it, one must feel at ease within one's self. But no man is an island unto himself. He lives with other people and therefore should feel at ease in relation to others. He should feel adequate and sense that he is on equal terms with others of his same age and background.

This primary need to feel adequate will express itself in many different ways. A group of scouts were planning to hike up the Indian Trail to the top of Five-Mile Mountain. A seven-year-old brother of one of the ten-year-old boys begged to go along. "It's a steep climb," his mother reminded him. "Oh, I'm old enough, and besides, Dad's going," the boy protested. The mother gave her consent; she wisely recognized that to refuse his request was to doubt his adequacy.

A child's sense of adequacy may often come from the sense of belonging and the assurance that he is contributing to the family. A little girl earned money by doing extra jobs around the house, besides her normal chores. She put her dimes away and when Mother's birthday came, she proudly presented her with an ornate comb. "I bought it with my own money," she said proudly. Her satisfaction directly resulted from the feeling that she was finding her place as an individual.

A twelve-year-old boy obtained a paper route and sought out odd jobs around the neighborhood, such as washing cars or cutting grass, in order to buy a bicycle. His father was able to afford it, but to the youngster it was a great sense of satisfaction and strength to have been capable of carrying through such a project.

If you are impatient with your child's efforts to learn, you may threaten his feeling of adequacy. Here are typical examples:

Mary, eight, wanted to accept the responsibility of keeping her room. As she struggled to make her own bed, her mother stood by impatiently. Naturally, Mary's first attempt was awkward and the made-up bed was lumpy and wrinkled. Nevertheless, she was happy and proud of herself. Her mother, however, was not satisfied. No sooner had the girl completed her efforts than the mother pulled the covers off the bed and proceeded to make it up again. She tried to soothe Mary by telling her that she was too young to do such things properly, but it is hard to conceive of any other act which would so cruelly undermine the girl's feeling of adequacy.

Edward, also eight, is a second grader. The school bus stops two blocks from Edward's house, and Edward wishes to walk that distance each morning and afternoon by himself. His mother fears that Edward may be run over unless she accompanies him. So every morning Edward endures the embarrassment of walking to the bus stop with his mother, while other children of the same age are permitted to take the trip on their own. After school, the mother waits at the stop to accompany Edward home.

Teddy is a bright, eager boy of seven. He is seldom permitted to play alone. When he rides his bicycle on the sidewalk, his mother walks by his side. When he plays ball with other children, his mother sits nearby. If he runs fast, she will warn him of the dangers of falling. When he plays simple card games with other youngsters, his mother sometimes takes the other children aside and asks them to let Teddy win a few games so as not to "hurt his feelings."

As a conscientious parent, you must repeatedly ask yourself whether you impose too many of your own wishes upon your child, whether you make all his decisions for him, whether you prevent him from doing anything of importance on his own. The child who feels inadequate may remain more or less dependent on others for the rest of his life.

So if you want your child to grow up as an individual who is emotionally well-adjusted and able to cope with the changing conditions of life, remember this basic point: He must have security and a feeling of adequacy—to have both he must feel that he is wanted.

CHAPTER TWO

Your Child from Birth to Two

Early Feeding Problems

The most important moments in your child's early life will be when he eats. They are important psychologically as well as physically.

During his first year, his greatest instinctual urge is to satisfy his hunger. He gains weight spectacularly and on his first birthday may weigh three or four times his weight at birth. Obviously, he should get enough to eat. Lack of sufficient proteins, vitamins and minerals handicaps his physical growth and affects his psychological development. A hungry child is an insecure child and an insecure child is an unhappy child.

Feeding not only supplies the food a child needs, but also satisfies his sucking reflex. But the two may not be satisfied at the same time. He may want to continue to suck after he has finished eating. To satisfy this urge he may take to thumb, finger or fist sucking, or he may suck some handy object such as a blanket or an old-fashioned pacifier.

Sucking is a baby's first real psychological pleasure—the exercise of a function for its own sake. He enjoys sucking for the same reason his father enjoys golf—it's fun.

There is no reason to deny the infant this simple pleasure, but it is well to prolong the feeding session so that he can suck for milk for longer periods. He will then come to associate his oral needs specifically with food. As he is weaned, his oral needs will become associated with a new way of eating, and so he will normally outgrow the sucking habit.

The manner in which the baby is fed also can affect his

psychological welfare. The pendulum has swung from breast feeding to bottle feeding and now is swinging back to breast feeding. Most pediatricians today encourage mothers to breast feed their babies if they possibly can do so. The physical advantages of breast feeding are few, but there are important emotional advantages for both mother and child.

During breast feeding, the mother can derive real joy from holding her infant close and feeding him through her body as she did during pregnancy. The infant senses the warmth of his mother's body and, when he lies snuggled within her arms, he achieves probably the closest possible similarity to his physical presence in her womb. If a bottle must be substituted, the mother should not fail to hold the baby in her arms while he drinks, much as she would do if he were being breast fed. The constituents of the mother's milk can be simulated or even improved by use of a proper formula. But there is no substitute for the love which every baby craves and needs.

How much and when a child should be fed are other important considerations. The laws and generalizations of the social sciences tend to be formulated in terms of averages. But individuals, including babies, are never just average. So the average formula and the average feeding schedule are just statistical regulations derived from averaging a group together. In reality, babies can vary as much as adults in their eating habits: some eat considerably more than others; some like to eat a little at a time, but often; some eat greedily and less often; others eat irregularly.

Most pediatricians now recommend that the baby be fed when he seems hungry, irrespective of the hour. In accordance with the old custom of schedule feeding every three or four hours, the baby woke up on schedule at night. Parents who forget schedules and feed the baby when he is hungry may learn, to their surprise, that he soon sleeps through the night without awakening them.

Inexperienced parents sometimes think that every time a baby cries, he is hungry. The tiny infant quickly realizes that crying brings attention. But it is possible to differentiate between the cry of hunger, of discomfort due to wetness or tiredness of position, and the crying demand for attention. Constant feeding and constant handling or cradling in the mother's arms are the beginning of spoiling the baby. He needs love, but not continual attention.

Toilet Training

The first stage in your child's development is known as the oral stage, because he is preoccupied with feeding and sucking. Psychiatrists term the second stage in the child's personality development the anal stage. During this period, elimination assumes a primary place in his awareness.

Urination and defecation are pleasurable acts for the child. He may play with his feces when the opportunity arises. He enjoys the feel of them and likes the smell. The overly meticulous parent finds this behavior unspeakable and unbearable and concludes that the child must be punished or shamed mercilessly and at length. In fact, such a parent may zealously train the child to regard the feces as bad, or filthy, and to consider his act an insult to his family. Such an attitude is unthinking.

If your baby at one time or another plays with his feces, as most children do, the best way to handle the situation is to clean up the mess without emotion or display. The child meant no wrong. He simply found something to play with and did just that. There is no need to punish or shame him.

The problem of toilet training is exaggerated by many parents. As a result of clinical experience, psychiatrists have for some time stressed that danger may be done to the child's emotional development if toilet training is given too early or too rigorously. Parents, in general, direct their whole interest toward the proper time at which such training should take place, when their concern should be placed, rather, on how the training is given and how the child reacts to their efforts.

Bowel and bladder training seem to today's typical parent to be of prime importance in child upbringing. Usually this period is regarded by parents as an unpleasant, even a dirty, distressing period to be endured and passed through as quickly as possible. The young mother is proud when her child attains proper toilet habits early. She would be shocked if you told her that she is using her child for her own selfish satisfaction without regard for his feelings or emotional development! Yet that is the cold truth. Moreover, a mother who boasts of a "clean baby" of eight to twelve months is simply deluding herself. True, a baby may have a predictable time for defecation and consequently appear trained. But the act is automatic before two or three years of age, one over which he has no control at this time. Normally, it is functionally impossible for a baby to control bowels and bladder at this early age.

The following plan is suggested to aid in toilet training: it should not start too early (the end of the second year or well into the third year is ample time to begin). If you do not become emotional about the training, but simply take it as a matter of course, your child will do the same. You should pet and praise your child when he voids or empties his bowels properly; when he does not, you must be completely passive without display of anger or annoyance.

To encourage your child to adopt proper habits concerning bowel and bladder function without arousing an undue emotional strain requires patience, understanding, kindness, and praise. Don't push your child too far; don't scold too much or ridicule him; try to understand his urgent needs. Praising his achievement can make the training easier. Your child should never be given reason to feel that his bowel and bladder eliminations are anything other than normal physiological conditions.

Parental mismanagement of toilet training can bring one of two undesirable results. The child may become rebellious and restrain his urinating and his bowel movements until he involuntarily soils himself or his bed. He may indeed restrain his bowel movements for several days, necessitating an enema or a laxative. The resulting discomfort only increases his resentment and makes him more determined not to comply with adult wishes.

On the other hand, he may be dismayed at his mother's displeasure when he soils himself. If he is insecure to begin with, the fear of losing her affection may make him try very early to comply with her demands. Soiling to him becomes a naughty, disgraceful act, and he makes every effort toward control. In later life this extreme effort to be "clean," to make his organs function on demand, to be rigorously in control of every bodily act in order to merit social approval, can lead to an overmeticulously "clean" personality, manifested in phobias (fears) and compulsions.

It is important to note in this connection the close association of the generative organs and the organs of elimination. This is a major reason for exercising care in toilet training. This close association is not only anatomical and physiological, but also psychological. Clinical experience with mental patients gives sufficient evidence that patients who have trouble arising from toilet training also have trouble with sex.

Genital Play

Many parents are disturbed by what they regard as masturbation in their very young children. They often become unduly harsh with the child in an effort to stop the practice. This play with the genitals is no more significant than the oral stage which preceded or may accompany this stage, in which the child played with its mouth by putting its fingers and every available object into it. The child makes no effort to conceal his genital play, because he feels no sense of shame or guilt. Parents should react with similar matter-of-factness. They need not be unduly alarmed, nor should they display revulsion. By showing their dislike of genital play they only stimulate the child's interest in his explorations. Usually the child will give up the practice spontaneously when he finds other interests beyond his body.

Your Child's Primitive Pleasures

At this stage, your baby laughs because he is pleased within himself. He plays though all the world may be sad. He smiles and gurgles independently of what goes on about him.

One often wonders at this spontaneous joy an infant shows. Many a mother who has heard her baby squealing with delight alone in an adjoining room has asked herself, "What makes him so happy?" He enjoys the things he does. He uses his sense organs and his motor powers in their primitive state and as sources of pleasure in themselves, before their use becomes, through learning and development, subordinated to his higher functions.

As adults we sometimes experience this primitive pleasure of sensory or motor function. The worker who sits at a desk all week feels a great pleasure on Saturday when he uses his muscles to beat a rug, mow a lawn, or walk around a golf course. He is conscious of the strength of his muscles, and feels a vague but distinctly pleasant sensation in using them. He may have an emotional and social satisfaction in a clean house, a well-kept lawn, or a low golf score, but he also has a purely sensory pleasure from muscular functioning for its own sake.

Adults sometimes also feel a primitive pleasure from the use of their sense organs, such as sight or hearing. The best example of enjoyment of these primitive sensations is probably provided by those adults who could not see or hear until an operation gave them this sense for the first time. One patient was blind from birth. Following an operation which gave him sight when he was an adult, he described seeing "many beautiful things," and enjoying them for themselves, although he could not identify them as objects he knew.

There is a difference between understanding through our sense organs and purely feeling with our sense organs, between doing something with our motor powers for a specific purpose and simply doing for its own sake. It is important for you to understand this point if you are to interpret the child's world from the child's point of view, and not the adult's.

When a mother wonders what her little one finds to be so happy about, she can obtain the answer only within her child and apart from her own viewpoint. For example, the baby enjoys the movement of his arms and legs. At first this is even less well-defined. Before the baby learns to kick one leg or move one arm, he moves his whole body. Although it may seem completely purposeless in an infant, it has a most fundamental purpose, i.e., to exist for its own sake. So the baby's first joy is of a purely sensory kind based on his own bodily functioning. Some of these sensory joys are almost eliminated as he grows to adulthood, some are partially modified, some are only slightly changed.

Some infant actions are of a purely reflex nature, as if the bodily part involved derived satisfaction solely from doing its job. These reflexes may also be essential to the infant's proper care. For example, two reflexes necessary for the intake of food, the sucking and swallowing reflexes, are present at birth. Also inborn is the rooting reflex. You can see this reflex in action by touching your baby's cheek with a smooth object. His mouth will turn toward the object, and his lips will open to try to grasp a nipple. This rooting reflex is one of the "sensory-pleasure-drives," which is entirely eliminated in adult life. The swallowing reflex is well preserved in adult life, although its importance can vary greatly. A medical syndrome found in adults and older children is that which is caused by excessive swallowing of air. These individuals seem to derive what we might now call a primitive or "unconscious" pleasure from swallowing. It is function for function's sake, carried to excess and not subordinated to more important needs.

Another interesting reflex present in the newborn is the grasp reflex. Place your finger over an infant's palm. His little hand will close over it tightly and will hang on with a surprising force. Many infants have such a tenacious grip that they can be lifted up in this manner; it almost seems as though the fingers can't resist the urge to grasp something just because they have the power to do so. In the few months following birth this grasp reflex is lost, and by the time your infant is six months old, he will be able to grab in a deliberate manner.

In New York City, not long ago, a father decided to develop his child's muscular abilities by placing a broomstick across the crib. The infant grasped and hung on while his father slowly raised him to a sitting position. This progressed until the father could raise the baby, who was clinging to the stick, to his feet and then lift him from the crib and keep him suspended in the air. One day the infant crawled through the window to the fire escape several stories above the street and slipped through the grating. As he fell toward the ground, one hand encountered an iron rod. Grasping it, he held on until his screaming mother ran down the steps and rescued him. To the baby it was just the game his father had taught him—but it saved him from serious injury and possible death.

When an infant is a few months old, he grabs everything. As he is set down in his crib, he clutches his daddy's tie. He grabs his mother's hair when she bathes him; sometimes he brings tears to her eyes before she can free herself from his pull. Sometimes he grabs his own hair and then cries because he thinks someone else is torturing him. At about eight months of age, he acquires the ability to use his thumb and individual fingers in a more precise grasp.

The need to grab follows the individual throughout his life. In later childhood it is coupled with other needs, such as inquisitiveness and daring. Even adults grab for something when they experience pain or clench their fists in anger; thus, there is a logical basis for the familiar expression, "He needs something to hold on to."

Many parents are not surprised at the physical pleasure their child derives from the activities that sustain life, basically because they are still familiar with such need fulfillments themselves. For example, they expect their child to enjoy eating because *they* enjoy eating. They expect him to be refreshed by a sound sleep because *they* are so refreshed. However, because of toilet training difficulties some parents have experienced in childhood, they regard the process of elimination as an unpleasant task; thus, in training their child, they take from him the natural pleasure he should derive from evacuating his bowels and emptying his bladder.

In addition to enjoying the things you enjoy—eating, sleeping, watching television, etc.—your child will take pleasure from activities that mystify you. He may derive great joy from pounding his hands and feet against the walls of his crib, pulling his sister's hair until she screams, squashing a caterpillar between his fingers, or humming or talking incessantly, whether anyone is present or not.

Such pleasures are normal for a child, for his first interests are concerned totally with himself. He is pleased by his own activity and by no one else's. He is pleased when drinking milk because it satisfies his sucking reflex, his swallowing reflex, his hunger pangs, and his grasping ability as he clutches the bottle. He is not in the least concerned with how hard his mother worked to prepare his formula or his orange juice. In fact, he takes no pleasure in her contribution to his comfort because from his viewpoint she has made none. His pleasure is all derived from what he himself does. He is a supreme egotist. Behold him—and marvel at the changes that must occur before he reaches adulthood.

Fortunately, other needs must also be gratified, and these gradually take the child out of himself. These basic needs begin to be apparent during the preschool period. They redirect the child's attention more and more toward the world in which he lives, and toward other individuals in that world.

The Years of Greatest Need

Your newborn must rely upon you totally. Certainly many young parents must often feel that their baby is just seven or eight pounds of "needs." With diapers to change and wash, bottles to sterilize, formulas to prepare, feedings and baths to give, in addition to all the other chores that a baby inflicts upon young parents, you may be excused for expressing the wish that he grow up fast. Won't it be wonderful, parents often think, when Junior is off to school?

But there are always at least two sides to a situation. Often it is only in later years that parents fully realize how much mutual joy and pleasure they experienced in administering to the needs of their young children.

The very helplessness of your infant can be a source of your own happiness. Moreover, he actually gives you something in return for your devotion to him. He does not barter his affections as adults sometimes do. What he gives is completely spontaneous—and is given whether anyone is present to receive his gifts or not.

One might briefly summarize a child's first two years by

saying that they are the years of greatest needs and greatest learning. The abrupt change from life in the womb to life in an ever widening world is certainly the greatest single change that happens to a human being. Happy babyhood years give back to the child the security and satisfaction of needs which the traumatic process of birth disrupted. These early years are the time of the child's maximum dependence; they should be the period when parents strive to provide a continuity of protection and security.

As the child grows, he will become less and less dependent and therefore will require less protection. Gradually he will discover his individuality and become a self-reliant human being.

CHAPTER THREE

From Baby to Child—Ages Three to Five

The Exploring Stage

The period of infancy lasts to the end of a child's second year. The preschool period then begins and continues until the age of five. During this stage, there are rapid gains in height: the average child will grow three inches per year.

Even more important than physical growth, however, is the personality development of the "preschool child." This time in which he evolves from cradle to classroom will present tremendous turmoil for him. Once he acquires a proficiency in walking, his development transports him from the dependence of infancy to the first step of childhood independence. As his parent, you will witness an interesting and complicated progression.

The average child begins walking with support at about twelve months of age, and without support at about fourteen months. Unlike speaking, which must be taught, the child walks whether he has been taught or not. His new method of travel brings him into personal contact with the world around him, and he develops an increasing inquisitiveness about that world. Previously, he enjoyed the physical acts of hearing, smelling, tasting, drinking, seeing, and even defecating. Now instinctive curiosity appears. He is not satisfied with the mere function of his senses; he wants to explore what he sees. For example, he shows more discrimination in what he eats. His mouth no longer pops open at the approach of a spoon to his lips; he first looks at the proffered food and may reject it by withdrawing his head or by pushing it away with his hand.

Of course, a young child cannot perform mental exploration as can his parents. He has neither logical ideas nor de-
ductive reasoning. His is purely a sensory exploration: he
learns about objects only by how they appear to his senses.
If he becomes acquainted with an object through one sense
organ, he will try to learn more about it by using his other
sense organs. This can lead to extremely odd behavior and
may even cause parents to erroneously suspect that their child
is abnormal.

The sense of taste is one which the child uses most often
in his efforts to learn more about everyday objects. Everything
goes into his mouth. He sees a piece of wood at the top of
his play pen. He finds it attractive. He feels it and notes that
it is shiny, smooth and hard. The natural thing to do next is
to put it to the test of taste. Everything must stand that test
—his father's shoe polish, his mother's purse, his sister's hair
ribbon, his brother's finger, his grandfather's tie. He learns
that some things taste good, some taste very bad, and some
have no taste. The maturing child also learns that some
things are not to be tasted—for instance, his brother's fingers.

His sense of hearing is also called upon to tell the child
more about objects that come to his attention. This explains
the attractiveness of a rattle. It can be looked at, chewed,
handled, and grasped, and it can be shaken to make a noise.
He loves to make noise: it is this need to explore with his
hearing that causes him to bang his foot against his play
pen, thump his sister's head with a handy ash tray, and knock
his glass against his plate. Such behavior is exploration at a
very young level, not perverseness nor a sign that he has
"old Satan in him."

He also wants to learn by touching. It is characteristic for
two-year-old children to repeat the phrase, "Baby see." For
them, however, to see usually means to touch. They can see
grandmother's new glasses, but they really want to explore
them by handling them. They plainly see their mother's vase,
but they must touch it to learn more about it; thus, ink gets
spilled, china gets broken, fingers get burned on hot toasters.
The frustrated mother says, "Won't that child ever learn?"

She fails to realize that her child *is* learning, in the only way he can.

You may tend to become frustrated as you watch your child eating. His fingers go into his milk, his soup, his vegetables. He sits with one hand dangling in his cup of milk and the other clumsily transferring cereal to his mouth. It will help you to bear the sight if you realize that your child must go through this stage in order to develop.

His eyes provide another classroom. Watch a two-year-old stare at a blank piece of paper or a piece of material left over from his mother's sewing. He turns it with his hand and contemplates it with his eyes. He is learning that he can tell the size of a thing by his sight as well as his touch. As he runs his hand over a colored page, he may be wondering why red feels the same as blue. He can see a difference. Why can't he feel a difference? So again he learns that there is a difference in sensations, and that some characteristics of things can be perceived by only one sense organ.

As your child extends his curiosity to other things in the world about him, you may find yourself becoming unduly upset. You probably will not become too excited when he puts his fingers in his ears to learn how deep they are, or in his nose to find where it goes. But when he removes some dried mucus from his nose and attempts to explore it by staring closely at it and examining its taste, you may wonder how any child of yours could be so crude! However, such exploration is necessary and, within limits, normal.

Your child will be interested in his products of elimination. He will carefully watch the process of urination and the result, and you should accept as natural that he will derive pleasure from the sight. Bowel movements are more complicated, but he can study the end product. And this he sometimes proceeds to do. The same senses—sight, touch, taste—are relied upon.

A three-year-old will also explore his genital organs and his anus. He is curious about his whole body, not just the depth of his ear or how far he can stick his tongue out. He is curious about his toes, his fingers, his penis, his anus and his navel, his "Adam's apple," and any other part that catches his attention because they all belong to him. If you permit him to explore these areas naturally, his curiosity will be satisfied and he will find other things to occupy his attention.

Motor Functioning. As your child progresses in the walking stage, he will make increasing use of his motor powers. As a newborn infant he moved his entire body with gusto, but without much design. Now his motor power takes on fuller meaning, and movement becomes another thing to be explored and tested. The grip of his hand is no longer a reflex which works automatically, nor is it merely a means of bringing objects nearer so that he may inspect them closely; now it has interest for its own sake. So he tests his grip by yanking the dog's tail, grabbing the bread knife, pulling his sister's hair, or, even more pleasurable, pinching her.

He may begin to frighten you with his daring. The world is rapidly expanding for him; he hurries about doing everything, trying not to miss anything. Instead of walking, he may try running, hopping, skipping, sliding. Climbing opens other avenues of exploration. The attic stairs, the back-yard fence, shelves of the kitchen cupboard, the neighbor's garage, the tree on the front lawn all stimulate his urge to know and the need to test his strength. You will rescue him from one escapade and while you sit lamenting, "What will that child get into next?" he is off to new adventures, to climb new heights, see new sights, hear new sounds, and test new strength. The TV set is no longer something that is simply watched; rather, it is something to bang with another object, something to climb and even to upset, if possible.

Destructiveness. During this period, parents often accuse children of being "willfully and deliberately destructive." Of course, children in anger sometimes break things, but never in the premeditated way suspected or done by their elders. Much of what parents consider to be willful destructiveness is actually a childish form of creativeness. A clock, after all, is much more interesting when broken down into its component parts. Think of what a child can do with the little wheels, springs, levers and sundry parts. The wheels spin like tops; the levers line up like soldiers; the springs make bridges. That these various parts once made a reasonably good clock is of relative unimportance. Little children feel no need of clocks. In fact, at bedtime their world would be pleasanter without them.

Parents often overlook the fact that children have no way of knowing the value of things. You give your child an empty box to play with. He destroys it and you don't mind. You can hardly consider him destructive when he happens to damage the box Sister calls her camera. Or you praise him when he helps you by carrying a few everyday dishes from the table to the sink. Why should you have hysterics when he does the same with your best china?

Often the apparent destructiveness merely represents a different point of view. A pretty doll with long curls and a lovely dress may look nice to you. Your three-year-old daughter may prefer to have one amputated arm to carry around in her pocket, she may prefer the doll without clothes on, or she may wonder what the head looks like without hair. She is not necessarily destructive—only curious, spontaneous and original.

Parents who buy expensive paints for young children usually feel disappointed when the paints are intermixed to become a dirty, grayish hodge podge. But the child is happy. First he dabs the colors around and admires them. Then his young mind may ask, "What if red is painted green?" So he proceeds to learn by doing. The end result may be various shades of ugly gray—to his parents they are drab and unstimulating—but to his vivid imagination they are as real as reds and greens. To him, his painting is as beautiful as if it contained all the colors of a rainbow.

The young boy with a wagon succeeds in removing a wheel and is overjoyed. Now he has two toys in place of one. He has a wheel which he can put on its side and spin like a top. He can roll it like a ball, or throw it like a discus. He was bored at times with his four-wheeled wagon. Now his three-wheeled wagon presents a challenge to him. He must find some way to make that wagon go. At any rate, he is not consciously being destructive, only creative.

During this period, when the little child develops from crawling to running, parents sometimes feel he has suddenly changed from a baby to a little boy. They are struck by his independence and explorations, his daring and imitations. He is a creature of contrasts. For example, a little boy, returning home from the circus with his father, called out to his mother, "Watch this!" Down on the floor he went and boldly crossed his legs behind his neck. His face was red, almost black, by the time his frantic parents unhitched him. His bravado gone, he clung to his mother in terror. He didn't try that again: he had learned something from his experience.

Thumb Sucking. Most parents seem to be convinced that by the time their youngster is three, he should no longer suck his thumb. Some parents may tolerate bed wetting, possibly because no one outside the family need know about wet pajamas. But it is embarrassing for many parents to see their three-year-old sit gloomily sucking during the Sunday sermon, or retreating to a corner with his thumb for comfort when a gushing aunt comes to visit.

In addition to embarrassment in the presence of others, parents are often concerned about thumb sucking because they fear that some great harm will be done to the teeth and mouth, thus spoiling their child's appearance.

There is no basis for these fears. The fact is that most children suck something as a residual after weaning. Not all suck their thumbs: some suck their fingers, some a blanket, a sleeve, or their mother's skirt. The natural explanation for this activity is that a child is born with a very active and powerful sucking reflex, which is practically essential for his survival. Otherwise he would be unable to draw milk from breast or bottle. This reflex is gradually taken over by higher centers in his nervous system and becomes modified in biting and chewing. But the child continues to associate much of his early comfort with sucking, for that was the time spent in the loving embrace of his mother's arms. It meant satisfaction of his greatest needs—hunger for food, affection and security. Therefore, in times of stress, the young child resorts to that which previously brought comfort. If the gushing aunt frightens him, if the Sunday sermons bore him, or if bedtime brings him loneliness, his thumb can give him solace.

The fear that a child will spoil his dental alignment by thumb sucking is totally ungrounded, according to the best scientific knowledge. To prove this, a researcher at the Merrill Palmer School in Detroit constructed many series of plaster casts of thumb suckers and of non-suckers. He established that when thumb sucking stopped before the child's second teeth appeared (at about age six), the suckers needed no more tooth straightening treatments than did the non-suckers. Thus, from a dental point of view, there is no danger to the child's teeth from thumb sucking before the age of six.

What is the best way of handling the problem of thumb sucking? Paradoxically, it is by not regarding it as a problem. A child who receives only mild attention in this matter will not do an excessive amount of sucking, although he may continue to do a little. He will probably outgrow the habit long before the age of six, especially if you don't turn it into a battleground by making him aware that you are overly concerned. As with toilet training, if he is permitted to realize that he has a weapon with which he can anger his father and frustrate his mother, he will use it to drive you to despair. He may do this purposely—to hurt you for hurting him in some way—but he will also do it as an experiment, to see again the surprising effect it has upon you.

He may also use thumb sucking to get attention, and it serves this purpose well. As a baby, his sucking needs—his need for food, in other words—enlisted your care four to six times a day. If he sucks his thumb now to gain attention, you should begin to consider that his sucking may be an indication of his need for more care and attention than he has been receiving.

The Demanding Stage

The young toddler is not as guileless as we have made him out to be thus far. He is not always the innocent victim of your inability to see things from his point of view. At about the age of three and a half, while he is still in the walking stage, your child also enters another stage—the demanding, or assertive, or "hell-on-wheels" stage. Although religious leaders tell us that our little ones are not morally responsible for their actions until they are about seven, the age of mis-chief is reached long before that time.

Like so many other things in life, the growth process of the preschool child operates like a pendulum. At birth he swings far to the side of egocentrism—that is, he is concerned solely and exclusively with himself. When he begins to walk and explore, he is forced rather moderately in the direction of society. Now in the assertive stage, he swings back to the extreme of egocentrism. Later, in the nursery school stage, he will swing back in the direction of society. And then there will be another movement back toward the self. However, as he grows and matures, the pendulum comes to swing farther toward others than toward the self.

The young child's desire to wander and explore and ex-periment is a source of fear, not only to his parents, but also to himself. When he begins to walk, he does not suddenly lose his desires for such essentials as food, warmth, love, security. Consequently, as a reaction to his own desires for self-reliance—desires which bring him momentarily away from his mother's apron strings—he now frequently returns screaming "Mama!" This is not the same timid cry of "Mama" he used to make. Now he calls "Mama!" with a tone of expectancy and demand. In short, he wants what he wants when he wants it and he will attempt to browbeat all who stand in his way.

At this stage, your child will make increasing demands for attention. The average youngster is a master of many tech-niques in order to achieve this end. He uses the natural coy-ness of his age to win from his parents their companionship and care. Although they strive diligently to give him love and attention, his demands at this age are almost insatiable. You may spend day and night trying to please him; there will still be times when he will scream in rage at what he considers to be neglect.

Your child soon learns by trial and error to recognize the various forms of behavior which bring him the most return. You should therefore remember this basic rule in dealing with his attention-getting devices: he will repeat those acts or series of acts which obtain the attention he desires. If he discovers that vulgar four-letter words bring a shocked re-action from his parents, he will repeat them for their at-tention-getting value and will stop using them when they no longer achieve the desired result. It is easier to state this principle than to apply it, however; it is necessary to know what motivates the child to do what he is doing. His ab-dominal pains may be his way of making you stay home from a party, for example, or they may be the first signs of an inflamed appendix. You cannot be sure until there is a pat-tern of incidents to indicate the former diagnosis.

Bed Wetting. While this habit usually has other causes, it may also be a means of gaining attention. Occasionally there are organic reasons for a child continuing to wet the bed beyond the age when most children stop. These reasons vary from *spina bifida* (hernial sac on the spine) to local infection and irritation. But organic causes are the exception. In most cases, bed wetting is caused by psychological factors. Of course, in this matter, each parent thinks of his child as the exception.

Most children stop wetting somewhere between their third and fourth birthdays. However, there is considerable normal variation beyond this range: many stop wetting by the age of two, whereas many continue to have difficulty until they are five. Bed wetting which continues beyond the sixth birthday, with no physical cause, may be called enuresis.

Enuresis is the result of an emotional disturbance. It may be the child's reaction to some unpleasantness: he retreats to earlier levels of behavior, such as thumb sucking or bed wet-ting. It may be stimulated by parental neglect, by parental severity, by the birth of another child who competes for the parents' affection, by moving to a new home, by the presence of a stranger in the home. How fear creates enuresis was demonstrated clearly in World War II. Bed wetting was al-most epidemic among children separated from their parents and home when London was evacuated.

Most frequently, enuresis is the child's way of showing hostility against one or both parents for some real or ap-parent wrong they have committed against him. Bed wetting may result from a parent who is severe and rigid, who looks for faults which he can criticize, who permits no show of anger on the child's part. The little victim of this parental dictatorship becomes tense and nervous by the unchildlike demeanor he must maintain to escape being scolded or whipped. His tension becomes the neurological mechanism which predisposes him to wetting his bed.

Usually parental wrath descends upon him anew for his breach of regulation. This only aggravates the matter, for the child's fear, tension and repressed anger are increased.

Assorted treatments are attempted. But scolding, denial of privileges, shame, ridicule—all fail to improve the situation. Then the parents take a fatal step: they coax, make promises, offer rewards. This only serves to convince the errant child that his parents are really concerned, and that he has achieved mastery of the situation. Just as he has longed for their understanding and cooperation, now they long for his. He realizes that he finally has a weapon with which to bargain for favors. Of course, enuresis does not actually *solve* his basic emotional problems or his parents' dilemma. With the professional assistance of a psychiatrist or an interested family physician, parents and child may be enlightened about their respective roles in causing the situation, which is truly unpleasant for all of them.

You probably can end the bed-wetting practice in its early stages by relaxing your controls, treating your child with more leniency and kindness, and giving him the attention he needs. But if the habit continues, without delay you should seek the professional assistance of a psychiatrist or your family physician.

A boy intensely loved by his mother but severely disciplined by his father continued to wet his bed throughout childhood and into his teens. This prevented him from doing many normal things; for instance, he could not go to camp with his friends. No physical cause could be found for the disturbance. His mother thought she solved the problem by setting an alarm clock to ring at midnight. The boy then went to the bathroom and wet the bed only infrequently. Nevertheless, he wasn't cured until he was fifteen, and then only with the aid of a psychiatrist.

Possessiveness. When the child is three or four years of age, he manifests his self-centered point of view in another way: he becomes very possessive. His cry, "That's mine!" may be heard from the back yard as he plays with neighborhood children. When the morning mail drops through the door, he yells, "Mine!" If a baby is born in his family, or even in a neighbor's family, he says, "My baby!" Psychologically speaking, this is truly the age where mine is mine and thine is also mine.

You can tolerate this phase if you recognize that it is an attempt on the part of the youngster to cope with the enormous world around him. It is a device he adopts for his own security. One might compare it to the attitude of the revolutionary, who finds it difficult to live in the world as it is and so decides to change it into "my world." Then he expects others to adjust to his way of doing things. The little three- or four-year-old is, in a way, staging an outspoken rebellion. It's difficult to live in the adult world, where everyone bosses and nags him and misinterprets what he does. Therefore, if he can gain enough of that world to give him the security he needs, he can live in peace and happiness.

To explain a child's behavior on the basis of one motive, however, is always hazardous. For instance, he could be expressing his discovery that possessions may be protected verbally as well as physically. At the time he was one year old, he laid claim to things by the clasp of his tiny hand. He pulled them closer for inspection and investigation, and as long as they were in his hands they were truly his. Now that he is older, he is often told that he must not touch what belongs to others in the family. Mother, father, brothers, sisters all impress him with their remarks, "Keep your hands off that. It's mine." So the word "mine" becomes a magic formula which grants him the right to use something as he wishes.

Boastfulness. Along with the three- or four-year-old's revolutionary spirit expressed in the word "mine" goes a great deal of boasting to compensate for what isn't "mine." Like some contemporary international politicians, he covers up what isn't favorable by loud claims about that which is. Father's success in business is minor compared to his own imaginary triumphs at play. His sister's mastery of multiplication cannot outshine his own illustrious feats of spelling. His brother's jokes are nothing to laugh at, but his own are extremely funny. In short, he can do anything better than everyone else, and everything better than anyone.

Boasting and belittling go hand in hand; indeed, they are one and the same thing expressed in a slightly different way. Boasting consists of elevating oneself above others; belittling, on the other hand, is a way of deliberately placing others beneath oneself. Since others have obvious merits, it is a means of praising oneself.

The child's boasts are often a one-sided affair with no implications relating to his father, sister, etc. One of the reasons for his boasting is because he wants to enter the world where others do things he secretly knows he cannot do.

As with possessiveness, there is usually a second motive for boasting, such as a new way to use words—another experiment to try, another mystery to solve, another lesson to learn. The child has formerly used one-syllable words to express his simple needs. Now, as he advances to bisyllabic language, he feels his increasing command of words. He discovers that "words are power" and he is determined to use their power to fill in the gaps in his world. Boasting is one very normal result.

Quarrelsomeness. Because of his possessiveness and his boasting it is inevitable that he should run into opposition. Others—parents, brothers, sisters, and playmates—are not always willing to let things be taken over by this particular three-year-old. Nor will they believe without question his wild, boastful claims. However, since his need to be possessive and boastful is important to him, he persists even in the face of opposition. This results in quarrelsomeness. Adults often feel that he is deliberately trying "to pick a fight:" the rebel's immediate reaction to this statement is to contradict or answer it with a boast. It is not merely for the sake of argument that he does this; rather, it is because he is trying to establish his place in the adult world which surrounds him. Perhaps if you can console yourself that such quarrels help him find his place, you will be able to endure them more stoically.

Negativism. The preschool child between the ages of two and five sometimes manifests that manner of behavior which psychiatrists and psychologists call negativism. This is the momentous time he learns to say "no!" and mean it. When negativism begins, he may shout "no" and emphasize it by stamping his foot, clenching his fists, shaking his head, and protruding his chin. He says "no" not only with his voice but with his whole body.

Oddly, this negativism frequently involves things the child really likes to do. If he is hungry and told to come to dinner, he may sulkily refuse. If he has been waiting all week to go downtown with his father, and now he is told to hurry and get ready, he may stamp his foot and say "no." When his older brother hears the ice cream truck and shouts at him to hurry and get some ice cream, he is likely to refuse. Yet in each case he will cry if he doesn't get what he has just refused. When he does not want to go to bed or refuses to come to his bath, his negativism seems entirely reasonable. But why does he refuse those things he desires most?

The most plausible explanation is that he is acquiring a new ability, that of refusal. He is so intrigued by his own new power that he cannot resist using it in spite of the unhappy consequences to which it sometimes leads. He exercises his power much in the same manner as the one-year-old heeds the urge to grasp things. The infant likes to close his hand over objects solely because he has the ability to do so. If the object is a knife, the hot handle of a pan, or a poorly placed electric plug, he may suffer considerably, but use of the ability itself brings him pleasure. So it is with the two-year-old's newly discovered ability to use his will. Agreeing with others hardly seems like using his will at all. But to use it *against* others—that is a real test of strength! Therefore, his apparent disobedience is not always the result of hostility, laziness, or other malicious motives that may be attributed to him. It may be only a secondary effect of his need to use his new power.

Jealousy. In the demanding stage through which the child is passing, he often shows jealousy toward his brothers and sisters. Some sibling rivalry, as this is technically called, is quite normal. It depends more on the child's phase of development than on any actual preference parents may show for other children. Sometimes a child of three years develops a jealousy toward another brother or sister and carries it into adolescence. It may even remain as a pathological influence when he becomes an adult.

This jealousy has a twofold object and is based on two fundamental needs. The two objects of jealousy are, of course, the younger children in the family and the older children in the family. The basic needs at the root of jealousy are the need to remain close to the parents for security, and the need to leave the parents and establish independence. Much of childhood—and of adolescence too—is spent in adjusting these two needs in proper proportion.

The need for security and support from his parents causes the child's jealousy toward his younger siblings, because the younger ones require more care and more coddling. Four-year-old Peter has a baby brother. When the baby came home with Mother from the hospital, Peter saw the infant as a wedge between him and his mother and father. His mother now devoted much time to the care and feeding of the newcomer, and Peter felt abruptly brushed aside. His father did not play ball with him much any more. Instead, Father stood over the crib and gave his attention to the new bundle of playfulness. Under these circumstances, one can hardly blame Peter for resenting the threat to his security. His new attention-seeking behavior and his jealousy toward the baby were quite normal reactions.

The way in which this jealousy is manifested varies according to parental attitudes and the child's own behavioral patterns. Peter displayed his by unusual sullenness and by frequent and repeated crying spells. Other youngsters might display general disagreeableness if they are afraid to express their negative feelings more openly. A child who is not constantly watched by his parents might show his jealousy by pinching the baby's toes until he cries, by sneaking away with the baby's bottle before he gets to drink it, or by taking off the baby's bonnet while he plays outside on the porch on a cold day.

Jealousy toward older brothers and sisters has a different cause. The four-year-old is not jealous of his ten-year-old sister even if Mother spends time sewing for her or Father buys her a watch. Such actions do not threaten his security and his bond of love with his mother and father. It is his need to be independent and to have new experiences, that causes his jealousy of older siblings. Tom's older brother goes to the movies but Tom must stay home; he resents his brother's privileges. John's sister stays up for "hours" and John resents having to go to bed much earlier. Edward's older brothers and sisters go to school every day and return with exciting tales about teachers, games and school incidents. These and multiple other apparent privileges make four-year-old Edward envy the exciting life that his older siblings seem to enjoy. He may manifest his jealousy by boasting in their presence, quarreling with them, destroying their possessions, teasing them, and reporting their misdemeanors to their parents.

The Nursery School Stage

After struggling through the turmoil of getting acquainted with himself and after beginning to get acquainted with the small world around him, the child now enters the final stage of his preschool development. Now he must get acquainted with those outside the family circle. He enters upon what we might call the nursery school stage.

This development, like all others in the child's life, calls for important and—to him, sometimes, terrifying—adjustments. It is indeed a great step forward. Until now, he has been wholly concerned with himself. Now he must learn to live in accord with children of his own age.

Of course, companionship with other children need not come only from attending nursery school. Many children's "nursery school" is the neighborhood sandpile, and their own back yard is their kindergarten. Nursery school is not limited to a particular place. It is more importantly a companionship with boys and girls of a similar age, who almost automatically have similar interests, similar concepts about life and the world. Parents, aunts, uncles, older brothers and sisters cannot provide this companionship for a four- or five-year-old child.

Some adults try to reach the child's world by using child-sized furniture in one or two rooms, or by playing children's games as if they enjoyed them. Such devices are artificial and are usually doomed to failure; there is no adequate substitute for your child's association with others in his age group, such as nursery school children, back-yard playmates, or small cousins who visit on week ends or holidays.

Your child will learn a great deal from these relationships. His first lesson in cooperation is something quite different from obedience. He gains more certainty of his own personal worth—based more on equality than on condescendence. He gains a better realization of the rights of others, based on a social code and less on the dictates of authority.

Your child has been busy since birth "trying out" the world into which he was born and now he has an opportunity to test other new situations. He made mistakes before by grabbing the butcher knife, by attempting to climb a tree, by biting his sister's arm. But from most of his mistakes, through trial and error, he learned something new. He will continue to err as time goes on, for he lacks the capacity and experience to weigh the possible outcome of each activity he undertakes; but he will also learn.

To be sure, in this world of playmates he will often learn the hard way. He sees a toy car and grabs it. At once he is set upon, and the result is major tears and minor bruises. The first few times this happens, he will rush home crying, and your first reaction may be one of outrage against the child who hurt your little Johnny. It is wise to question Johnny—remembering that you are not likely to get the full story—and explain to him the significance of what happened. If you act calmly, you will shorten the period of trial and error learning, and help to decrease the number of nose bleeds.

With his new friends, your tot has the first thrill of true companionship. He discovers the joy of playing games with others. Moreover, these children are of his own age and welcome him. No one orders him to "get lost" when he joins the group.

When your child enters nursery school or joins a neighborhood group, he obviously takes a step away from the restricted family circle. Therefore, this is, as we have suggested, an extremely important step in the preparation for his eventual maturing. It is not an easy step—in fact, it is probably even more difficult than his first physical step. More unknown factors, and thus more fears, surround this experience.

When your child first started walking, you tried to allay his fears and give him confidence in himself. You recognized that he would have to do most of the work himself—that too much help would have delayed his walking. Now, as your child takes another major step, it is helpful to bear this principle in mind: give enough help, but not too much. He must not lose his security, but at the same time he must gain self-confidence. As with all such general principles, concrete application is not as simple as it sounds.

For instance, your child will be especially subject to fears during this time; the fact is that a delicate balance should be maintained between the security of his homelife and the insecurity of leaving the family circle. As the insecurity involved in making new contacts increases, his security at home is moderately threatened. He tries to gain greater security at home to balance his new insecurity. But the time will soon come when he establishes sound relationships with others outside the home and gains new security in these social relationships.

Since fears are a dominant feature of insecurity, your child may become afraid of the dark, of dogs, of being alone. During this period, fears may be manifest in bad dreams or nightmares. He may sleep restlessly, toss about and grind his teeth. If you regard these fears as symptoms of insecurity and try to increase the child's confidence in your love and protection, they will usually be short lived.

A result of the child's increasing independence outside the home is his increasing independence inside. His new interests make obedience more difficult. It is one thing to follow your instructions and to pick up his toys when there is nothing else to do. It is quite a different thing to collect the toys when his neighborhood buddies are calling for him outside. So he rebels against authority.

Temper tantrums often increase sharply at about this time. His temper may flare up when his desire to join his companions is thwarted. Incidentally, this remains a constant source of resentment throughout his youth. Tantrums may also serve as an attention-getting device and occur most often during the nursery school age because the first feelings of independence and of resentment toward authority are coming to the fore at this time.

Your child's imagination, which is probably at its highest development . . . during this period, may also provide you with some anxious moments. Some children experience difficulty in separating the world of actual events from the world of fantasy. As a result, they often find themselves in trouble concerning stories they tell. One mother expressed horror and shock whenever her child came home with entirely false stories. She spanked the child for lying. This reaction was really uncalled for and out of place, for it only tended to confuse the child. The mother might well have waited patiently: in time, her tot's imagination will become less extravagant and take its proper role among his mental powers. Meanwhile, it is a new power he has discovered—and what he discovers he must test.

Not all the small child's wild stories are reports on his imaginative wanderings. Some are lies—deliberate concealment of the truth. As such, a lie is intended to convey an idea different from what the liar knows to be true. This is exactly what the lying child aims to do.

It has been said that the first real lie that each person tells is born of fear. Without question, fear is a frequent cause of lying. The threat of punishment hangs heavy over some children. If you spank your child when he says he tore his pants while climbing a tree, he may claim the next time that he does not know how his pants got torn.

Using words to say what is in one's mind is one of the most remarkable of man's accomplishments. Many children are fascinated not only with their ability to use words but also with the possibilities of deceiving adults by means of them. They enter into deceit as if it were a game and get the same kind of pleasure from its success as they do from any other game.

Certainly, neither of these forms of lying can be considered malicious. The former is a matter of expediency to which, unfortunately, many adults succumb. The latter, in childhood, is usually a matter of fibbing; in adulthood, of course, it can become malicious and may be done deliberately for monetary, political, or other gain.

How you handle your child's lies, as well as his displays of possessiveness, quarrelsomeness, his tendencies to boast and to tell wild stories, will, to a large extent, determine his personality in later years. It would be helpful for you to remember that as the preschool child develops from infancy to that first maturity of school life, he goes through many phases: in each, he must come to grips with specific problems. Most of these problems, as we have noted in earlier pages, are related to his new powers and feelings, with which he must learn to deal. He may blunder repeatedly; he is certain to make mistakes; he is likely to seem "impossible" at times. However, through all of these turmoils and troubles, your child is learning to deal effectively with these awakening abilities and feelings. Equally important, he must be allowed and even helped to acquire effective and socially acceptable ways of confronting and controlling his emotions.

If parents are rigid and perfectionistic, if they do not tolerate minor lapses, they may be responsible for lasting character problems in their children. For example, there are parents who will not permit their child to express hostile feelings toward his toys, his playmates, his brothers and sisters, and, of course, toward them. The child cannot express his anger, but he nevertheless continues to feel it, more deeply than ever. A patient once reported that as a child, she had felt angry toward a young playmate because of a minor grievance. She had been unable to express her anger and had not even wished to admit it to herself. For more than four years the anger grew and made her life miserable. Only when she was finally able to get it out of her system did she feel at ease.

When children learn that anger, lying, quarreling or any other defects cause their parents to withdraw from them, to consider them bad or shameful, they will be afraid of their own feelings, since they begin to assume greater significance than they ordinarily would in a normal situation.

Consider, for example, what happens when anger becomes associated with loss of love and security. The child's next step is to repress or deny his angry feelings. He cannot stop anger any more than he can stop hunger pains in his stomach when he has missed his lunch. But he can relegate these feelings to an unconscious level. There they prowl about, seeking some worthy victim.

Other emotions may also be frustrated instead of being put to good use. If you frown upon your youngster's curiosity, he may fear his own experimental tendencies. If you turn sex into a forbidden subject, he may form all sorts of barriers against the normal expression of this drive in later years. There are many and various ways in which emotions can be frustrated and perverted and finally imprisoned in the unconscious mind, where they work havoc with mental health.

CHAPTER FOUR

Your Child Becomes an Individual

His Need to Do Things

After your offspring reaches the age of four, approximately, he ceases to be a baby and enters childhood: now he wants to be recognized as an individual, and to be dealt with as one. This development of the personality will continue for the rest of his life. He feels, thinks and acts in an *individual* manner, not just like *any* little child. Tommie suddenly announced after a short time in kindergarten, "I'm not Tommie, I'm Thomas." To him the name Tommie represented the baby he had outgrown. Such a reaction is common.

We have seen how the infant needs, above all, a feeling of security. He also has a need for a sense of adequacy, which will increase as he gets older. New problems confront the child during these years, and, in turn, these problems create a new group of problems for the parents.

His desire to do things to prove his powers may conflict with what you know to be best for his welfare. But it is well for you to realize that he needs to feel that he is an integral part of the world around him and that in his own personal way he is contributing to its structure—in short, that he "belongs."

An elderly man handed the evening paper to his wife and pointed to an item which reported that a group of boys, their grandson Bobby among them, had been arrested and fined five dollars each for swimming naked in the river. The grandmother admitted she knew about it.

"Did you give him the five dollars?" the man demanded.

"No, he didn't ask for it," the grandmother said. "He arranged for a loan from the druggist and is working it out in the drugstore on Saturdays."

The grandfather wisely remarked, "Good. He's learning that he must pay for his mistakes." The boy profited by handling his own problem.

What factors tend to threaten your child's feeling of adequacy, his sense of "belonging"? One is the parental rejection mentioned earlier. Another factor is what we call "sibling rivalry"—the rivalry between children in the same family. A child who is treated as less important in any way than a brother or sister will feel inadequate and jealous of the preferred sibling. A little girl who had been petted and spoiled because of frequent illnesses was unhappy when her little brother arrived. All her parents' praise and attention seemed directed to the son. They loved the little daughter no less, but now had no time to caress her. Her old attacks of croup became more and more acute, and her parents once more directed their attention to her. They finally realized that the girl's sense of hurt brought on these terrifying attacks. When they shared their affection equally between their children, the attacks ceased in severity.

Parents who consciously or unconsciously show favoritism toward one or more of their children indirectly relegate the others to the role of second raters. The latter are certain to feel a sense of personal deficiency. Two brothers quarreled continually. The mother usually favored the younger one and berated the older boy for lacking consideration of his brother. The father paid no attention until the din became unbearable; then he punished both of them. In either case the older boy—who rarely was the aggressor—held a deep resentment toward his parents because their unfairness always made him feel personally inadequate.

Self-Expression

Another need which emerges into the foreground when a child approaches his fourth year is the need for autonomy—the right of self-government. As he matures, his abilities to express himself continually increase. He becomes more and more aware of the world, the people in it, and the role that conversation plays. So he begins to express his opinion on topics which his elders are discussing. He likes to have his choice considered when a vacation is planned. Often he insists that he be allowed to select which clothes to wear: this selection draws attention to himself as an individual, or expresses a rebellion against clothes his mother prefers.

Little girls at this age emancipate themselves from babyhood by decking themselves out in long dresses purloined from their mothers' wardrobes. They scuff along in high heels, wear women's hats at a rakish angle, may even wear face powder, lipstick and perfume.

The youngster has his own way of responding to provocations and his own emotional expressions. He is cognizant of his power to communicate with others and of the effect speech and behavior have upon them. Try to encourage these attempts at self-expression so that he may gain confidence in his abilities and easily establish a reciprocal relationship with the external world.

Also during this stage, the child discovers that he has the power to do or not to do. He feels an inner drive for independence—a desire "to be a man." This urge may conflict with the commands of parents or teachers. Even though he knows that punishment will follow his disobedience, he may decide that the exertion of his will is worth the pain.

The superego is being fashioned at this time. Let us pause to consider Freud's concept of the human psyche. Introducing new terms, Freud presented in his *The Ego and the Id* a topographic-dynamic view, dividing the human psyche into three departments, the id, the ego, and the superego, each of which influences the others.

The id consists of inborn, instinctive strivings, mostly sexual in nature, which blindly seek satisfaction. The id serves as a reservoir of energy, supplies the driving force to the mental life of the individual, and motivates him to do what he pleases when he pleases.

The ego is the conscious part of the human personality, the source of collective perception, conscious thoughts, conscious feelings and voluntary movements. It is this developing ego which first makes us recognize the child as an individual. He not only knows what he wants; he lets us know what he wants and insists upon getting it. His ego is that which may cause him to say "I won't."

The superego, as coined by Freud, represents the censor, or conscience. Whereas the id is an inner drive to gratify all desires, good and bad, the superego is the watchman over the id and the ego. It consists of all the experiences and reactions of the younger child, and his recognition of the "must nots" imposed by parental authority and by the barriers encountered in group living. Natural acts, such as swimming in the nude, thus come to be regarded as minor crimes according to social and legal standards. The superego, or conscience, passes judgment upon our conscious and unconscious thoughts, feelings and actions.

The superego prevents the individual from doing what is morally wrong and also familiarizes him with the demands imposed by social standards. It is not morally wrong to eat with one's fingers, for instance, but our social laws condemn it. A child learns very early that it is a sin and a crime to steal, but the superego goes further than the law; it makes the *desire* to steal a sin. The superego is that part of the personality which is a result of environmental influences and dictates to the individual the reasons for correct behavior.

As a parent, you can do nothing about your child's id, because it is instinctive. But you can affect his ego and his superego, mainly by discipline.

How to Discipline

In order to discipline properly, you should realize that your child's awareness of what is "right" and what is "wrong" comes slowly. By the time he is three, he understands that there are some things—like vases and lamps—that he should not touch. He conforms to the rules because obedience assures the love and approval he must have.

After the age of three, most children become less pliable. They disobey deliberately; they develop strong likes and dislikes. As they reach five or six, they acquire a degree of social adjustment. They learn that certain acts are not to be committed. They want to please so that they may be loved, but often they do not know that they are being naughty.

When the youngster reaches school age, he learns new sets of rules, directed not at him alone, but at the group; all must comply. Disobedience and rebellion on his part single him out as unacceptable.

Some adults—parents and teachers—discipline a child as they would train a puppy. They expect him to obey implicitly, coming "to heel" on command. A child who is trained in unquestioning obedience may make a good soldier, but rarely will he be successful as an independent citizen.

Discipline is necessary because a child has not yet learned the meaning and consequence of his behavior. Unless his asocial acts are corrected early, he may incur disapproval, even punishment from society in later years. There are six basic principles to bear in mind concerning discipline. You should learn these principles when your child is an infant, since you will be applying them throughout his childhood and youth:

1. *Keep in mind your real reason for punishing your child.* In attempting to improve his conduct and teach him to respect the rights and feelings of others, try to act calmly and reasonably, not in a fit of emotion. If you examine your role thoughtfully, you will realize that the child's future welfare, not your personal whim or dislike, should dictate the appropriate punishment.

Punishment can be of two general types. Positive punishment consists of spanking, slapping, or sending him to bed. Negative punishment consists of depriving the child of some privilege or pleasure as a result of his misbehavior. He may be deprived of candy, entertainment, play privileges, toys, or weekly allowances. Youngsters react individually to these various forms of punishment, and you can observe which type is most effective with your child.

2. *Make the punishment appropriate to your child's age.* Until he is about four years old, it may be necessary to punish him physically because his mind has not developed to a point that will enable you to reason with him successfully. If you

discover your child playing with electric wiring and the electric outlet, for example, you must spank his hands and clearly point out to him that he must not do it. As the child grows older, physical types of punishment should be discontinued.

No good is served if the punishment is beyond your child's ability to understand. Jimmy, a bright four-year-old, loved to visit a couple who lived next door. One day when they were having a snack, he joined them and ate cookies and milk. Then he said with a sharp look, "Do you know what I'm going to do?"

The man detected mischief in Jimmy's manner and said quietly, "Whatever it is, you hadn't better do it."

The boy gave a sudden yank to the tablecloth and sent the dishes crashing to the floor. The man arose, took the little hand firmly in his big one and led him to the door. "Get out, and don't come back for a week."

Every day Jimmy confidently knocked on the door and asked, "Is it a week yet?"

Finally, when the week was up, Jimmy came bounding in and cheerfully asked for "sumpin' to eat." He hadn't the least remembrance of what his offense had been. I would not have been surprised if he had yanked off the tablecloth the following week, for the punishment was entirely too subtle for a four-year-old to comprehend.

3. *Your punishment should fit the offense.* A child has a strong sense of justice. If his sentence seems too severe, his resentment and rebellion may make him repeat his act in defiance. A little girl "followed the leader" over a barbed-wire fence and tore her stocking. At home she confessed what she had done and was slapped for being a "tomboy." Feeling like a martyr, she ran back to the fence and, after removing her stockings, climbed over again, this time cutting a gash in her leg. The fact was discovered when she was undressed for bed. Fearing more punishment, she said she fell; therefore, her parents' overly stern attitude contributed to both disobedience and lying.

One day, as a mother was preparing her four-year-old daughter to meet an expected guest, she jerked her in the process of dressing her. The little one slapped back. The child was shut in a closet for what seemed an endless time. An adult who perpetrates such a cruelty should taste the horrors of being confined in a tiny, dark space. This is not punishment, but torture.

Your authority as a parent should be exercised in such a way that the child recognizes and accepts its justice. Authority unwisely exercised—and exercised without love—becomes a symbol of restraint, and those in authority become a symbol of the bonds that enforce obedience. An example of authority unwisely exercised is that of a mother who tied her little boy by a rope to the stove leg when he was "bad." No offense of which that boy was capable warranted his being treated like an animal.

If your child accidentally falls and spills his milk on the living room rug, or accidentally breaks a window when he's playing in a yard, it is hardly a matter for punishment. He may be made to clean up the milk as an adult would have to do, or in some way help to repair the window, but he should not be scolded or punished. He simply does not deserve it. If a child uses a dish his mother has forbidden him to use, he is being disobedient. If he breaks that dish, he deserves punishment. However, a four-year-old is probably not aware of the difference between his mother's fine imported china and the dime-store dishes he sees broken accidentally every once in a while.

One type of parent chooses to threaten the child by saying that she will call the policeman or, even worse, the "boogie man." Another type of parent watches, hawk-eyed, every one of her child's acts and warns that God will punish him in hell for minor transgressions. Children respond to such threats in one of two ways: they learn to dismiss the threats as meaningless and then, of course, the mother loses her major weapon of controlling the youngster; or, they develop terrifying fears and look upon God as an overly stern Father who is more to be feared than trusted. In later life, they may desperately need assurance as to the mercy and goodness of God. Because of the insidious threats they received, as youngsters, from their parents, they may find it extremely difficult to obtain that assurance.

Recently I had as a patient a boy, aged nine, who had become so terrified of the dark that he had extreme difficulty in getting to sleep at night. He feared that because of his sins—really not sins at all, but rather the normal actions of a boy his age—he would be severely punished by the Almighty. Another boy reached the point where he confessed his sins to the priest on Saturday but felt unworthy to receive Communion on Sunday because he might have offended God unwittingly by committing some minor offense. A five-year-old girl, who was attending a Sunday School, was so impressed by a sermon on hell and damnation that she could not get it out of her mind. Because of her one-sided introduction to the idea of punishment for sins, she displayed psychotic tendencies even at this early stage.

A child should be *severely* punished only in those cases where his actions may seriously endanger his own or another's health or life. For instance, he should be severely punished if he tries to eat various medicines—pills, tablets, etc.—or if he plays with fire or electrical fixtures. By severe punishment, I mean both physical punishment and the deprivation of privileges. True, the child does not realize the consequences of his action when he stuffs a few pills in his mouth, perhaps as he has seen Mother or Father do. Nevertheless, the danger to himself is so great that he must be prevented from repeating such actions in the future.

In determining the kind of punishment to mete out to your child, you will do well to remember that undesirable behavior is more likely to result from overseverity than from overleniency. Some parents, who cannot tolerate normal uninhibited children, act as dictators, with a definite blueprint of what and how a child should be. They forget that each child is different—an individual in his own right.

Bob is twelve years old, yet doesn't go to school. He wakes up every morning nursing a cold, is tired, feels dizzy, and is inclined to nausea. Sometimes he seems to be critically sick; once he was even paralyzed. He has been in the hospital several times and has had all the tests medicine has devised in the last fifty years. Results showed that he was suffering from no organic disease, but from an illness apparently psychological. Investigation proved that when Bob was three and four, his father regarded him as an overly sensitive child, one prone to accidents, and therefore had tried to "break" him of his tendencies. What could Bob do about his parent's strictness? He had to concoct a disguise that would keep him safe from punishment. His disguise took a form that fully protected him from his severe father.

In this explanation, one may frequently find the motive behind soiling, bed wetting, thumb sucking, fingernail biting and the development of tics, or habitual contortions of the face. A parent can hardly hold a child responsible for these apparently automatic acts or physical diseases, yet is often greatly annoyed by them. Thus, as in Bob's case, the child was able to express his aggression against his father, but was not held responsible for it. If he had been treated more leniently, he probably would not have needed to express such aggressive behavior.

Ill-advised punishment may also result in the temper tantrums of the typically "spoiled" child. Coddled and allowed to do as he pleases, this child can neither understand nor accept correction. When some situation necessitates absolute obedience, his aggression mounts and bursts forth in a temper tantrum. He screams and kicks, bumps his head against the floor, or even punishes his beloved doll or puppy as an expression of his resentment of authority.

4. *Make certain of your facts before you punish.* Sometimes you may misinterpret a child's actions and treat him unjustly. The importance of disciplining your child with a spirit of justice is vividly demonstrated by an example I encountered recently. A little girl was very close to her father. One day, when Dad was home from work, he called to Susan and asked her if she would like to take a walk with him.

"But you'll have to hurry," he said. "I'm leaving now."

The girl hurried downstairs and she and her father went off arm in arm. For almost two hours they walked through the woods, enjoying the beautiful sights of nature together. When they returned home, Susan's hand was still in her father's. However, Susan's mother began berating her, then turned to the father. "It is your obligation to spank Susan," she said. "She absolutely disobeyed me. I told her she must not leave the house without cleaning up the toys in her room. And just look at the room—it's a mess."

Without a word, the father removed his belt and gave the girl a thrashing. Susan wanted to tell him that she had begun to straighten up her room, when he suddenly called. She had to choose either to go with him or to straighten up her room and she did not want to miss the opportunity of enjoying a walk with Daddy. After the spanking, Susan went to her room without saying a word. But the injustice of the punishment rankled deeply.

From this occurrence, we can also draw another important moral: a parent should never punish a child in blind fury. All too often, children have what to them is a perfectly logical reason for acting as they do. If you try to learn the reasons for their actions, you may conclude that your youngster did the proper thing after all. Or if their reasons were unjustified, you have the opportunity to discuss them and to point out why they were wrong. In this way, you fulfill the basic purpose of discipline—to help your youngster avoid repeating his error in the future.

"It isn't fair" is a common complaint of children of four years and older. They dislike favoritism, but they resent injustice. While a spanking is most unwelcome, the child accepts it and forgets, if he knows he was naughty. But undeserved punishment is long remembered and resented.

An unmarried aunt, who was visiting in a home, was liked by the little daughter but disliked by the son because she always complained of his noise. One afternoon, a picture of this aunt was found on the table, with a hole punched through the nose. Only the girl had been seen in the room that morning, and despite her protests of innocence, she was switched. Many years later, when she was an adult, she said to her mother, who was very ill, "Mother, I didn't poke that hole in Aunt Nora's picture." Her mother gasped, "And you held that against me all these years?" "No," her daughter replied, "but I remembered it and I want you to know I wouldn't do such a thing."

A child usually demands fairness for himself; often he forgets to *be* fair. It is hard for him to learn that what's fair for him is fair for others. Jane was playing at Mary's house when a spat arose. "Go home," Mary said. Jane went, much hurt. The next day, the quarrel forgotten, Mary went to Jane's house, but she soon returned home. She said indignantly to her mother, "It's unfair of her. She told me to go home." Of course, Mother had to explain exactly what fairness is.

In line with the importance of punishing justly is this precept: don't punish your child twice for one offense, by bearing grudges, reviving old offenses, or harping on touchy subjects. An offense paid for should be forgotten. The slate should be wiped clean each time.

5. *Your child should understand why he is being punished*. Punishment which he cannot understand has a destructive, rather than a corrective effect. A little boy and his sister were having a gleeful time. The maid, left temporarily in charge, heard their tittering and tiptoed into the kitchen to see what they were up to. They had opened the refrigerator and devoured almost a quart of strawberries. The angry maid whaled both little ones. The boy accepted his punishment with little outcry and turned to his play. The girl resented being whipped for having fun. Opening the refrigerator and taking food had no connection, in her mind, with the spanking. She had done it often when she was hungry, and not been punished. Therefore, she related the punishment to the strawberries. For some time thereafter, she would not eat strawberries; her parents could not understand why.

If your child asks why he is not permitted to do a certain thing, he deserves a better answer than, "Because I said so." A little girl's mother told her she could not join some boys wading barefooted in the flooded streets. When the child asked, "Why not?" the mother replied, "You heard what I said." The girl did not go wading, and the mother probably concluded that she handled the problem in the right way. But unexplained denials and unexpected punishments do not prepare boys and girls to meet new situations. They have no basis upon which to know whether an action will be approved or not. They may have doubts concerning parental approval, but they take a chance. A boy was dared to walk the railroad ties of a bridge crossing a wide river. Fear of falling into the river, fear of a train that might come along, and fear of parental punishment if someone tattled could not equal his fear of being a coward, and he accepted the dangerous challenge.

A child may rebel against the thwarting of his desires and cry out angry words of hate, or may even strike the parent. The severe punishment which often follows such behavior is meted out as though the little one were capable of controlling his feelings and reactions. The misunderstood punishment brings, not a desire to be good, but a feeling of resentment and a desire for revenge. Only when a child is old enough to be expected to exert self-control is he old enough to understand why his outburst is not acceptable behavior.

An infant should be expected to react emotionally. When he reaches childhood, his emotional control should be trained according to the rate of improvement he individually is able to achieve. His infraction of parental rules should not be judged at the adult level.

6. *Your punishment must be consistent.* You should not let your child believe that he is being punished according to your changing whims. Yesterday his naughtiness brought only a rebuke from you; today he is spanked for the same offense. Playing his noisy locomotive through the house yesterday went unnoted, and in fact you were glad your boy was busy and in sight; today his racket proves exasperating and you threaten him with a stick. No wonder he is confused! A youngster sees no consistent element in punishment dealt out at the arbitrary will of his parents. One day they love him, the next day they don't. This means insecurity to him. He has no standard to guide him.

Even greater insecurity occurs when the child becomes a pawn between the different disciplinary systems of the two parents. The youngster soon acquires a cunning and goes to Father for some permission his mother will deny, or perhaps already has. It is important that each parent agree with the punishment meted out by the other. Sometimes, of course, the mother may feel that a father's punishment is unduly harsh. A father may feel that the mother is basing her discipline of the child on an incomplete knowledge of the true facts of the case. Under such circumstances, there may be disagreement, but it should never be thrashed out in the youngster's presence. Otherwise, he gets confused in his loyalties to his parents.

I remember an experience from my own boyhood illustrating the importance of being consistent. I had done something wrong and was told by my father that I must go to my room and would not be permitted to have any food that day. In the afternoon, my mother arrived at the door of my room with something for me to eat. I recall that I reacted angrily. "Aren't you ashamed to bring me food after Father said I was not to have any?" I asked her. To me, more important than food and drink was the need that my parents act in unison—that there be no disagreement between them in the upbringing of their children.

Youngsters have a keen eye and ear for inconsistency. Recently I had as a patient a girl whose mother complained that she never came when called. After the mother left, I began to speak to the patient alone. She turned to me angrily.

"My mother told you I wouldn't come to her whenever she called," she said. "What she didn't tell you is that she calls two dozen times when she doesn't really want me. All I hear all day long is, 'Dorothy, where is this?' and 'Dorothy, where is that?' Sometimes she says, 'Dorothy, please come downstairs for a moment.' I come downstairs and Mother is outside chatting with a neighbor. She may chat for fifteen or twenty minutes, expecting me to remain until she returns."

The story in *Aesop's Fables* which warns against "crying wolf" too often is a lesson every parent should learn; for unless your child can believe in your consistent behavior towards him, you will find—as did Dorothy's mother—that he will no longer heed you.

In this regard, try not to underestimate your child's powers of observation and his ability to form solid conclusions from what he observes. For example, a teacher announced that because a boy had been talking in class he would be obliged to remain after school for three days. When three o'clock arrived, however, the teacher remembered that she had other appointments. She reasoned that if she detained him after school she would also be punishing herself. So she conveniently forgot about keeping him after hours. He ran out to play and told all his classmates how he had "put one over" on her. The next day, the teacher could not understand why it had suddenly become so difficult to maintain order in the classroom.

Parents sometimes attempt to interfere with a teacher's discipline and normal duties. Instead of agreeing with the teacher, they side with the children, forgetting that discipline is ineffective without continuity. For example, some parents are determined to have their children obtain high marks. When the teacher, after careful analysis of the child's capabilities and extensive examinations, gives the youngster a "C" instead of an "A", the parents are outraged—not at themselves for failing, perhaps, to supervise their child's home studies; not at the child himself, perhaps for repeatedly talking in school when he should have been listening and learning; but at the teacher. The child hears the teacher criticized at home and cannot understand why the teacher must be obeyed at school.

If your children are to be assured of your love and of their acceptance as members of the family group, and if you are to be accepted by your children as directors of their behavior, you must establish a child-parent relationship, built upon a consistent, mutual love and understanding; a shared appreciation and respect for each other's individual rights and privileges. Only through such shared respect does the child learn to respect the rights of those outside the home.

As imitators, children learn more from example than from commands. The white lies parents tell, or ask their children to tell, give a poor grounding in honesty. The insincerities and emotionalism of parents rub off on their children. A mother I know was shocked to observe her little girl berating and spanking her doll; she had not realized the effect of her own outbursts of temper.

Your child should be led, not driven. The sole purpose of discipline should be firm guidance for proper conduct. It should be a help in developing strength of character and personality. Discipline should be a part of the socializing process which builds a better world through good citizenship. Discipline designed merely to keep a child from making a nuisance of himself is not constructive, and can be destructive. Lack of a moral code and proper standards arise both from overleniency and overstrictness and also from an inconsistency that swings from one direction to another.

Teaching Your Child to Accept Disappointments

How to deal with frustration is one of the most important things any individual must learn in order to achieve a well-adjusted personality. All of us are frustrated often; in fact, we ordinarily undergo minor frustrations every day of our lives. We are frustrated when we run for a bus and the driver closes the door in our face; or when we dial a number on the telephone and find that the person to whom we hoped to speak is not at home; or when a competitor secures the business we had hoped to obtain for our firm; or when our candidate for public office is defeated by another. However, simply because we do not get our way, we cannot expect the earth to discontinue rotating on its axis or its inhabitants to stop going about their normal affairs. When we are frustrated, it is we—not the rest of the world—who must make the adjustments.

It is necessary to understand, from early childhood, that no individual—not even the mightiest ruler in history—has ever succeeded in having all his wishes fulfilled. All of us have wishes we want gratified, but sometimes, in order to enable another person to have his way, we should be willing to deny our own desires.

Our frustrations will often be involuntary. Because we, as human beings, have failings and shortcomings, we cannot always obtain the justice to which we feel we have a right. From our days in the crib until we enter the business world, we discover that life does not always proceed along the route we would prefer. So too, your child, from his earliest days, should learn to accept disappointments. From this experience he will acquire the ability to deal with major disappointments of life instead of escaping from them.

Learning to cope with frustration is an almost automatic process in some homes. The child may observe that the mother never has enough money to buy a new dress. He may notice that his father fails to get promoted. If his parents react with the determination to work harder so as to merit a promotion, the child will most likely accept the thwarting of his own desires as a similar challenge.

Often, however, parents display bitterness about such things in the children's presence. The youngsters hear how other people always seem to have things their own way; how Mrs. Smith has ample funds to satisfy any whim which enters her mind; how Mr. Jones does little or no work but invariably gets promotions and raises. This kind of training does not enable the child to accept disappointments as a normal condition in life, and eventually he will feel that he is being discriminated against.

I often see cases where the inability to handle frustrations remains with individuals all their lives. At the age of forty or fifty, some adults manifest temper tantrums that we usually associate with the six-year-old. Some men—including those in high places in business and the professions—kick a chair or table when another person disagrees with them over matters of business procedure.

Recently I had in my office a thirty-year-old woman who sought my advice about some family problems. To understand the nature of the problems more thoroughly, I asked her a question concerning her own background. She refused to answer. I told her that I had to have an answer to help her. She felt cornered and thereupon proceeded to fall to the floor and hold her breath until she was blue in the face.

I walked into my outer office, where her husband was waiting. I told him what had happened, and he suddenly grew pale. "We must go right in and help her," he said. "She has these fits at home too."

I stepped in front of him. "I would rather not," I said. "Her fits and temper tantrums have only one purpose. She will try them only when someone is present to see them and become worried. The next time she throws a tantrum, go about your business as if nothing has happened. She will soon give them up as a means of getting her own way."

I returned to my office after a few minutes. The woman was sitting up, calmly smoking a cigarette. I told her that if she chose to throw a fit in my presence in the future, I would leave at once until she had completed it. She never had another in my company. Of course, this treatment should have been extended to her twenty-five years before.

You should not try to protect your child from all failures and disappointments, from every hardship and pain, for from his failures, as well as his successes his knowledge increases. From his frustrations he learns that not all of his whims can be fulfilled, and that rebellion is often futile.

If his failures and frustrations are attended by your understanding and love, these experiences will not be traumatic— that is, they will not produce a lasting hurt. He will accept disappointments without deep conflict. And through these experiences he will learn to accept his responsibilities as a member of society. He will become a healthy, wholesome individual.

The "Normal" Fears of Childhood

Your child's fears are a very special problem in his personality development. In fact, his development can be determined or conditioned to a great extent by the emotion of fear.

Fear in itself is not abnormal; there is a place for it in human life. It is not uniformly harmful, nor is it completely useless. It is rooted in our instinct for self-preservation; thus, it is a natural impulse and necessary for existence. It does not necessarily paralyze effort or inhibit achievement. Used properly, it creates a caution against, and avoidance of, the physical and economic dangers of life. Sometimes our fear of failure, for example, does not deter, but rather abets, our efforts to succeed, and spurs us to action. Therefore, it can be a valuable asset.

Unfortunately, not all fears are appropriate and serviceable for the individual. Some are obsessive, paralyzing, and disorganizing to mind and body. For example, a pathological fear that is out of proportion may destroy your peace of mind, cause unhappiness, and drain your body energy.

Children are practically fearless when they are born. Virtually all the fears which they manifest are brought on by their contacts with the world. Many fears are taught by their parents, and are actually necessary. For example, the mother teaches her child not to play with matches because he may get burned; not to talk to a strange man on the street because he may be kidnapped; not to take candy from a stranger because he may be enticed into an unwholesome situation.

The mother also instills fear by example. In a thunderstorm, she trembles and hides her head in a pillow. Her four-year-old sees her and does likewise—and perhaps never completely loses his fear of thunder for the rest of his life. One mother had a deathly fear of mice. She climbed upon a chair and screamed whenever she suspected that one might be nearby. Her son grew up to be a burly six-footer and a rugged football player. By introducing a toy mouse into the dressing room, however, his teammates could unnerve him sufficiently before a game so that he could not play.

A child also develops fears as a result of his own experiences, without regard to the example of others. For instance, a youngster who almost drowned at the age of five found it extremely difficult to learn to swim: memories of his earlier experience kept disturbing him. A child severely bitten by a dog may fear animals all his life. One who falls from a window may fear even moderate heights as a man; adults who have had severe falls in childhood may exhibit a fear of high places.

Many fears result from the young child's vivid imagination and are obvious in his play. He may be a cowboy, an Indian, a steamboat or a plane. He may be in the sky or below the sea. His imagination usually develops faster than his intellect, and because of this lag in intelligence and understanding, he may apply all kinds of real and fancied dangers to himself. He may be thrilled by perils he invents but successfully overcomes, or he may be terrified by his fancied dangers.

For one little boy with a very active imagination it was a nightly ordeal to climb the dark steps of his home to an even darker bedroom. There the swaying tree branches made menacing fingers on the wall or tapped a threat upon the windowpane. A shapeless garment on the wall or chair betrayed the presence of a burglar, or possibly a murderer. Every night the lad hurled himself into bed and pulled the covers over his head, hoping for swift sleep to release him from his terror.

Nightmares are also a fairly common experience of young children. These fears, which come out of the child's subconscious in his dreams, are always related in some way to his own experiences. He might have seen or heard something that frightened him. Foremost of these agents of fright are horror-filled comic books and adventure programs on television. Much long overdue publicity has been recently devoted to the impact of comic books on the mind of the young child. Even the child who professes to scoff at such horror tales may be affected adversely. At night, when his subconscious comes to the fore, the fears may assume a terrifying reality.

Nightmares may also serve to disguise the child's fear of physical or perhaps spiritual punishment. Frequently in back of such nightmares is a repressed desire to do something which would inevitably bring punishment. It can be an aggressive act, such as breaking a window of a despised neighbor, stealing candy, running away, or indulging in juvenile sex play. In sleep these forbidden "drives" are allowed free play and result in anxiety, which produces the nightmare.

How to Make Your Child Less Fearful

It is important for you to recognize that your child's fears are very real to him, however unreal the actual danger. They cannot be cured by ridicule, scolding, penalizing, or by being ignored. He must be assured that there is no threatening danger and that he has the protection of his loving parents.

Wherever possible, remove the causes of fear. For instance, children are often afraid of the dark, of being shut in a closet, or of being lost at night. The ordeal of going to bed in the dark may provide needless suffering for him, and does not necessarily make him brave. An installation of a tiny night light to guide him to his room, or to the bathroom at night, will probably dispel his fear.

Keeping in mind his ability to understand, explain that his imagined fears have no real basis. If he suffers from nightmares, screen his reading matter very carefully. In addition, make certain that he does not view television programs or motion pictures which may upset him. And, of course, refrain from instilling by your own example any fears in his mind above and beyond those necessary for his own well-being and safety.

In some instances, a child is afraid because he feels that he is unequal to the situation at hand, or because he feels within himself a basic insecurity. If he is customarily treated as a coward or a weakling, it is not easy to convince him that he is as capable as any other youngster to meet each struggle in life. Bewildered by stresses he does not understand, he does not know how to face a new situation or how to escape. Overprotection may have poorly prepared him for making decisions and meeting responsibility; or, overdemanding parents may have chilled his spontaneity and made him timid in the face of trouble.

Excessive fears are evidence of mishandling of the child, a lack of understanding or an ignoring of his emotional needs. His emotional instability should be recognized early and treated with love and understanding. He should not be coddled, but he must be loved; he must learn the value of responsibility, self-control, and getting along with others. Most of all, he must have a deep respect for moral laws.

Fear of the wrath of God and eternal punishment may deter children, and some adults, from committing suicide. Such fear however, does not cure unhappiness, feelings of unworthiness or guilt, or the desire for escape. The child who believes that God is a Father who loves and forgives the sinner, the child who takes his fears, temptations and griefs to the Father, is unmarked by disappointments and deprivations. Secure in His love, he feels no need to strike out against the world.

Sex Problems

Sex can easily become a major problem at this stage unless the parent handles the subject properly.

During this period, masturbation is almost universal. It may stem from various causes. It may be a carry-over from the infantile habit of playing with the genitals; or, it may be due to the fact that the child is lonely or depressed and seeks compensatory pleasure in a situation which others cannot take from him—masturbation; or, he may experiment as the result of an unsatisfied interest in "the facts of life."

Nearly every child has some kind of early experience with the other sex. This usually reflects nothing more than normal curiosity. Frequently, upon talking to five-year-old children, I discover that they have had a sex experience. Often this experience merely involves viewing each other's organs. Sometimes it consists of mutual masturbation.

You should not become unduly disturbed if you discover that your child has indulged in some activity of this nature. He has no reasoning to instruct him that such behavior is objectively immoral. You should, of course, explain to him why he should not indulge in it. But by treating curiosity about sex as a normal thing in childhood, you will avoid the more serious error of making it a hidden and a shameful thing in later years.

I know of one case in which a mother found her five-year-old boy with a girl in the cellar of her home. The boy and girl were undressed, standing several feet apart and merely looking at each other. Thirty years later, the man told me of his mother's reactions:

"The look on her face was one which I had never seen before, and never saw again," he told me. "Mother looked as though she had seen me killed before her eyes. She gave me the worst beating of my life. I was bruised and black and blue all over my body, and was forced to remain in bed for a week. I could never understand what I had done to merit such extreme punishment."

Of course, this mother practiced brutality. The children

were not aware of any wrongdoing. They were no more curious about this subject than they might be, for instance, about the inner workings of a watch.

A young child is interested in everything he sees; this includes every part of his own body. Therefore, his sex education should proceed along with his training in physical hygiene. He should learn to name correctly the external parts of his body and their functions. He soon notices that his father differs from his mother—Dad goes to work; his lap is hard; his hair is short and usually straight; unless he shaves, his whiskers sting. If he sees babies bathed, he may note the presence or absence of what he has learned is his penis. All of this curiosity is normal, and is not necessarily evidence of sexual interest.

He asks innocent questions as a means of learning. His early question, "Where do babies come from?" should be answered adequately according to his age and understanding, but always truthfully. Later he will ask how the baby is born, and this question too must be answered truthfully. Gradually he learns that there must be a father and a mother; that the embryo must be fertilized just like the embryo he has seen in the egg, but unlike the chicken which the hen keeps warm until the egg hatches, the tiny baby remains warm within the mother's body until strong enough to be born.

Your child will accept all this information without excitement or emotion, if you remain calm and unembarrassed. But youngsters who have been told that a stork, or a storm, or a doctor brings babies, are confused when inadvertently they learn the truth. They distrust their parents because of their deceit.

Special teaching in this subject should be given to little girls, whereby they may learn social rules. Just as they learn not to wipe their noses on their dresses, or break wind in public, they also learn not to expose their bodies or their panties. Teaching girls respect for the privacy and sanctity of their bodies should come early. If they are proud of their femininity and instructed in modesty, girls will not permit "pawing" by venturesome boy or predatory man.

Adequate and timely sex instruction is the greatest single

deterrent to sexual misdemeanor. Of course, sex instruction is quite ineffectual if the child has received no previous training in self-control. Those who point to statistics and say that sex crimes have increased with the advent of sex instruction miss this very point.

But we cannot blind ourselves to the fact that today sex is revealed boldly on stage, screen and in all forms of advertising. This can scarcely be classified as sex instruction; it is sex allurement. To offset these influences, from the very beginning your child's sex instruction should include the idea of self-control, practiced in accordance with the moral law. He should know that sex is part of God's plan for men and women, and that it must be used in conformance with the Creator's purpose.

CHAPTER FIVE

The Personality of Preadolescents

The "Golden Age" of Childhood

As your child enters the preadolescent age of about six years, he will exhibit noticeable personality changes. This preadolescent stage is a resting period during which mental and physical development proceed more slowly, as though in preparation for the accelerated mental and physical growth in adolescence.

Parents are delighted and relieved when their formerly exasperating youngster suddenly becomes a sweet little child, more obedient, more reasonable, less argumentative. This change is a natural growth in his personality, which comes with an increasing awareness of the interesting world around him. Usually when adults speak of the glorious happiness of childhood, the freedom from responsibility and the unawareness of adult worries, they are remembering the restful plateau of the preadolescent period. All too soon for parental comfort there comes an abrupt ending to this blissful era. For the age of puberty (about eleven) introduces a new and turbulent period in which there will be appalling changes in their child's behavior.

Development of the Conscience: The child from six to eleven has reached the age of reasoning. By now, in most instances, he knows what is "good" and what is "bad." He obeys commands, not only because punishment follows disobedience, but also because if he disobeys he is doing wrong. Sometimes he may obey grudgingly, because experience has taught him that obedience is more comfortable and because the reprisals he feared as an infant are still threatening. Another factor which aids the development of his conscience is his discovery that the gratification of desires that are "wrong" brings him little happiness.

Knowledge of what is right and what is wrong is not inborn. It must be acquired by careful, proper training. The child acquires patterns of behavior at home, at play, and at school which fit him to live amicably within a group that widens as his environment enlarges. Although he may never lose the notion that he is the most important person in the world (to himself), he begins to grasp the idea that other people are important too. He discovers that the only way he can get along with these other important people is to make frequent concessions to their wishes. He may learn this difficult lesson by the acquisition of a black eye, a scratched face, pulled hair, or torn clothes. If it is not learned at age six, it may have to be learned at age twenty-six, when the person realizes that he cannot make or keep lasting friends by being overdemanding.

You can develop a strong conscience in your child by giving him an ethical code of conduct to live by; most of all, by letting him observe that you too possess, and live in accord with, your own conscience. Some busy parents consider it sufficient to give their children a well-kept home, good clothes, food, and medical supervision. They think that because they are good, well-accepted people, their children naturally will be good. But a child is neither naturally good nor naturally bad. Therefore, he must be trained to know which is the right way, lest in choosing between two pathways, he select the wrong one because it seems more attractive for the moment.

Children are imitators. A parent who tells "white" lies should not be surprised if his child fibs to get out of a predicament or avoid punishment. Unless a parent is entirely honest, the child will feel no pangs of conscience when he yields to the temptation to steal something. The Smiths came out of a restaurant and the father chuckled because the waiter hadn't charged enough. A few days later, his son put a leaden plug in a pay phone and thought himself smart when it worked. Your child will develop little respect for a neighbor's property if he sees you throw trash over the fence or reach through and take some fruit. If you punish your little boy for saying "damn" and "hell" and use the same words yourself when you are angry, he will be confused and resentful.

Discovery of Sex Differentiation: During preadolescence, boys and girls note a difference in the social behavior demanded of them. Usually, little girls play with dolls and doll furniture, and boys have bikes and mechanical toys. And woe to one of the opposite sex who touches their possessions!

Chores they formerly shared together are now differentiated. The girl helps with the dishes and makes the beds; the boy mows the lawn and washes the car. At this age, a girl is as strong and as capable as a boy, but a line between "soft" and "hard" jobs is often drawn. Children take a firm stand on this subject: the boy says boys don't wash dishes; the girl refuses to wash the car and get dirty. In dozens of other ways, different patterns are set up for each sex.

There are many separate must-nots and must-dos for boys and girls. Sis loves to play ball, but running and hollering aren't ladylike. Even if her mother allowed her to play with boys, they would drive her away. In their earlier stage, boys and girls may have played contentedly together in sandpiles and waded in the water. But if Sis tags along now, she is ordered to beat it. If she lingers, she may even be chased away with sticks or stones. She can't understand why she's not permitted to join exciting games, she does not realize that such treatment helps, in large part, to develop her feminine personality.

For their part, girls gather in groups, deride a lonely boy and pretend to detest him. However much they like to play with boys and resent being "little ladies," they do not want boys to play with them. They may even mock one whose mother has taught him to be more polite than others of his age.

The boy who willingly pulled out his mother's chair at the

table may begin to feel silly; when he reaches adolescence he may refuse entirely, due to the fact that he is becoming more conscious of his masculinity and thinks such conduct is unmanly. Even though it is a nuisance for him to wipe his shoes on the doormat and wash behind his ears, he does both because everyone else does. But if he is "sissy-polite," his pals snicker at him and his self-esteem is hurt.

This awareness of sex differentiation explains why the preadolescent boy often protests against dancing school. He might really enjoy the rhythm and whirling around the room, but to bow to a girl and ask her to dance with him and then to thank her afterward—that is too high a price to pay. She may be the girl next door who made a face at him yesterday, or the girl who out-spelled him at school. It doesn't matter; at this age he doesn't like girls, period. All of which is his way of accentuating the masculine aspects of his personality.

Social Laws and Taboos: Your child's personality is, to a great extent, influenced by the culture in which he grows up. Social requirements demand that he make specific adjustments and also teach him to accept these, in time, as necessary and proper. He learns that certain acts aren't polite, are harmful to himself or others, or may even be against the law. Since he desires to be a conforming member of society, chances are that he will not feel thwarted, rebellious, frustrated or revengeful if he is taught that gratification of certain desires is taboo because it violates social law and custom.

Your child will make many mistakes, of course, before he learns which acts are socially acceptable. If he exchanges clothes with another boy, he should learn that he cannot dispose of these clothes as he pleases. He may also discover that a family anecdote is no one else's concern, and therefore should not be told outside the home.

Taboos which children must respect and adopt vary with different cultures and social classes. For example, fighting is usually frowned upon by the upper classes. Parents may interfere in quarrels before the fight starts, or as soon as one begins. But when lower class boys argue, they may be urged by their parents to "put up their dukes" and fight it out. To be licked, it is reasoned, is not half so bad as being a coward and taking an insult.

In upper-class surroundings, we often encounter a boy who is never allowed to release his anger, who must always be a perfect gentleman. He may be filled with a smoldering resentment and hostility. Unless he can work off his rage in harmless ways—by whacking a punching bag in the gym or by beating a drum in an orchestra, for instance—he may seek cruel ways of getting even.

Little girls, without regard to economic and social class, learn early that girls are not supposed to fight. Scratching, biting, and hitting bring severe punishment. They may release their anger, however, by making faces or saying hateful things.

Girls tattle more often than boys. In fact, tattling violates the code of most boys and they have contempt for a squealer. Often tattling is prevented by the threat, "You tell on me, and I'll tell on you." The threatened one is not always sure that something can be tattled on him, but he dares not take a chance. This device is common between brothers and sisters. Children often refuse to tell of abuses inflicted upon them; they may think such reporting is tattling, they may be loyal to some person, or they may fear reprisals for telling. The adult who carries tales is often despised by other adults, just as the boy who tattles loses face with other boys.

The tattler is even despised by the person to whom he tattles. Little Willie injured his back as an infant and wasn't allowed to play with boys; they "might hurt him." At ten he was a lonely crybaby. Brighter than most children of his age, he showed contempt for other boys, whom he called stupid dumbbells, and they in turn detested and mocked him. To retaliate, Willie tattled constantly. One day he told a new teacher that Sam was chewing gum. The teacher told Sam to throw his gum in the basket and never to chew gum again in school. But he also ordered Willie to write on the board a hundred times, "I am a tattletale." If this punishment taught Willie that our society rejects the tattler, it was a low price for him to pay.

The Challenge for Parents

The preadolescent years are the most challenging for a parent, for this age provides the richest opportunity for establishing the mental health of the growing child. His experiences at the beginning of this stage have been few and brief. He is ignorant of life and its promises, difficulties, and perils. He is also pliable and eagerly responds to affectionate guidance. Now is the best time to train him for a way of life; in a few years, when he becomes an adolescent, he will turn away from his earlier dependence and will resent guidance and authority.

Unfortunately, delinquent and neurotic personalities are also developed in this preadolescent period. They are made to flourish by lack of proper guidance, denial of affection and security, improper parental deportment, or by a disrupted home.

The development of personality should be a gentle molding into a fine character, not a hammer and mallet chipping of marble into some figure the parent wants to fashion. A child should be made to feel that he is an individual and an important part of the family; he should not feel that he is merely a possession of his parents, bent to their will, blindly obedient. Yet how often we see parents attempting to push their children along some carefully prearranged path.

One little girl's parents never read anything but the evening paper. The girl was avid for books, but they liked to spend their evenings playing games and considered reading a waste of time. Once they took their daughter to a poorer section of town, where an acquaintance lived. The house was unpainted, its porch was propped up with bricks, and holes in the windowpanes were stuffed with rags. Here, they said, lived a person who would not work and who wanted to do nothing but read. Thus, the girl's natural and normal interests were thwarted by her parents, who doubtless thought they were doing the right thing.

Often a parent whose wings were clipped by his own father and mother may want to fashion his child into what he himself wanted to become, forgetting the unhappiness and frustration such treatment brought him. Or a man who has won success in business may set up a place in his firm for his son, disregarding the boy's special interests as revealed by his hobby or collections. Just kid stuff, he thinks. He insists that his boy prepare to follow a prearranged career. The son may be denied training which might make him a successful artist, musician or scientist. Eventually he enters the trade or profession of his father. His success may be mediocre; he may be a complete failure. Of course, it is then too late to begin the studies which should have started even before adolescence.

Howard's father was a middleman, buying produce from farmers and selling it to grocers. A keen buyer, he soon built up a successful business. He looked forward to the time when his son would help him. But even as a boy of seven, Howard showed a deep interest in chemistry. His father cared nothing for Howard's budding talent. When Howard was graduated from high school, he was offered a scholarship to college, and also a full-time job. His father saw no use in a college education and persuaded the boy to take the job.

Howard's heart was not in this type of work and he was fired. He failed also in his father's business because he disliked interviewing customers. So Howard drifted, worked parttime, and dabbled with some interesting ideas regarding chemistry, but this ended in a blank wall; he had no education to enable him to go further. Given encouragement as a boy, he probably would have become a success in the field in which he was interested.

Howard's younger brother suffered a similar fate. He wanted to be a civil engineer, but his father took him out of high school to help in the business. When his father died and he assumed responsibility, he lacked the ability and desire to adjust. Ultimately, he failed.

If your child shows certain aptitudes and interests, you should seek to bring out the best that is within him. Your guidance should help him find a way of life, not just a way of making a living. He will be happiest if he chooses a career in which he is interested and in which he is most proficient, not one in which you would like to see him.

The power of parents' attitudes in forming a child's personality is vividly demonstrated as regards racial, religious, or class prejudice. Children are born without prejudice. If they are not taught it by parents or others, they will play with other children without regard to color or other differences. Only when parents or older youngsters introduce ideas of prejudice do children practice these attitudes.

Proof of this fact was demonstrated in parts of the South, when Negro children first began to attend schools with whites. The white children in many instances invited the Negro children to sit and play with them. But when adults began to protest against integration, the white youngsters realized that they could hurt the others by taunting them about their color.

A person who displays prejudice is consciously or subconsciously telling himself, "Here is a person who is inferior to me." He must constantly reassure himself that others are inferior—whether that actually be true or not—because in reality he suffers from deep feelings of insecurity. Almost invariably we find the most prejudiced persons among the most poorly educated classes.

I once had a neighbor who was more upset about the "Colored Question" than anyone I have ever met. He was obsessed with the notion that Negroes might move into the community and he missed no opportunity to harangue other neighbors about his views. He became a thorough nuisance. This bigot was the most ignorant person in the area. He had had only a few years of elementary school training. At the root of his prejudice was the fact that he knew he was an ignoramus; only by denouncing Negroes could he satisfy himself that there were others who were inferior to him. He chose to ignore the fact that many Negro people have exceptionally superior intellects and would grace any community; if he had acknowledged this, the entire apparatus of hate he had built to protect his ego would have crumbled.

Prejudice takes many forms. One highly educated young woman came to me and said, "I love someone and would like to marry him, but I can't. He is a Catholic, and my father simply does not regard Catholics as full Americans. If I married this boy, I would break my father's heart." Sometimes snobbery works in a reverse way: if the opportunity arises, underprivileged children will mistreat a youngster from a privileged family. I have also encountered instances where families with four or five children, regardless of their basic qualities, are looked down upon. The reason? "Nice people don't have more than two or at most three children," one man once remarked to me. "A couple with more than that number are really little more than animals."

Prejudice usually harms the one who practices it. Rich little Laura was taught to associate only with nice girls in good houses, and never to play with a less-privileged child, whose parents were poor. Now and then Laura played with Anne, who lived in an alley nearby, but to make certain that no one saw her, she always played in Anne's yard. In her adolescence, she tried to overcome her snobbishness, but her prejudices by now were so ingrained that it was impossible. As an adult, she refused to help in community work, because although she gave financial support, she could not bring herself to have contact with lower-class people. She was a maladjusted person.

As a parent, you must realize how easy it is to transmit your own prejudices to your child. He will copy any uncharitable remarks you make against those with a different race or religion from your own. A girl of nine enjoyed walking home with a cheerful, light-colored Negro girl. One day, as they passed a large clubhouse, a Negro woman of darker complexion came to the open window and chatted with the Negro child. The white girl told her mother of the incident and was rebuked for being friendly with a Negro girl of the servant class. From then on, the white girl took a different way home —and never forgot the lesson in intolerance.

Class distinctions are impressed upon girls more than upon boys. Socially ambitious parents exert influence upon their daughter's choice of friends; they want her to know the right people and later to marry well. Sometimes they train her so rigorously in this area that she becomes unpopular and is left out of parties.

Other attitudes of parents which shape the child's personality can vary from complete laxness to utter harshness; or, they can strike that happy medium—sympathetic guidance with praise for good behavior.

The overstrict parent who makes the child walk a chalk line and punishes him for every step over the line, who considers every query, "Why must I?" and every protest against commands as impudence, fails to build up a standard of judgment or a sense of responsibility within the child. The child does not ponder whether an act is right or wrong, but whether he will be punished if he is found out.

A parent may be overstrict because his own parents were overstrict. Often an adult will say, "When I was your age . . ." and insist that everything be the same today, disregarding new customs and ideas.

When considering the unhappiness that parents may cause by their overstrictness, I recall the case of Katherine. Her mother and father, strait-laced people, had been married for ten years and had settled down to a narrow, self-centered life. Then Katherine was born, and while they were proud of their fertility and loved the child greatly, she upset the home's equilibrium. Katherine could not please her parents; whatever she did was wrong. If she lifted the curtains to look out, she was mussing them; if she lay on her bed during the day, she had to remove the top cover and remove her shoes; she had to stand at the sink whenever she ate cookies, so that the crumbs wouldn't dirty the floor. Her room was inspected daily and all her letters were read, no matter how carefully she hid them. If she laughed heartily, they considered it loud and impolite; if she expressed any opinion which opposed that of her parents, they thought it ridiculous and saucy.

It was only when she went away to college that she finally found happiness. With this taste of freedom, she accepted a job far from home as soon as she graduated. Her mother called her ungrateful for leaving them alone. But Katherine never returned. Her parents' overstrictness literally drove her away.

On the other hand, many parents are often overindulgent. They let the child get away with anything. The causes may be disinterest, resentment of the strictness they suffered as children, the deprivation they experienced in childhood, or too many outside interests which intrude upon the proper amount of time they can spend on supervising their children. Regardless of the reason, the indulged child will be selfish and demanding and will face difficult problems of adjustment in school when he learns with shock that he is no more important than any other youngster. He may be aggressive and in continual quarrels with his schoolmates; or, he may be shy and cling to his parents, the only ones, he thinks, who appreciate him.

The Mother's Direction

The mother affects her child's personality in numerous ways. The mother incapable of controlling her child may be heard to shout, "Stop that!" or, "Didn't I tell you not to do that?" or, "Didn't you hear me tell you to come?" Still the child pays no attention. The mother may then use wild threats of punishment. The child who is heedlessly annoying, but desires her affection, may become apprehensive about losing her love. Or if the child is unable to please her, he may be filled with fear and show a resulting nervousness that may become deeply rooted in his make-up.

A mother unhappy in her marital relations may lavish excessive love upon her little one, seeking love which her husband denies her. In one typical case, a daughter responded entirely. She never was able to break away and felt secure only in her mother's affection and protection. When she married, she insisted upon living near her mother; when her mother became divorced, the daughter insisted that they live together. In another case, the daughter never married. Mother and child clung together, with few intimate friends. When the mother died, the young woman felt stranded and desolated.

A boy smothered in mother love never quite grows up. He remains dependent upon his mother, seeking her opinion in all matters. Often his own married life is unhappy because the competition between wife and mother is too great. The little girl who is "the apple of her father's eye" may be similarly dependent. Unless the mother makes each child feel loved and wanted and accords him the same love given to his brother or sister, he may become jealous of the other children; this can lead to great unhappiness and maladjustment.

Sometimes the first-born child is made the family martyr. He—or more usually, she—must care for and protect the younger children and exert some authority over them. Another hazard for the first child is that when a second child arrives and requires all the attention he enjoyed earlier, he may feel deserted and rejected by his mother and deprived of his rights and privileges. In some instances, a younger, preschool child may be the one who feels deprived and underprivileged, because he is not allowed to go to school, must go to bed earlier, and often must wear hand-me-downs.

However much she tries to be impartial, a mother tends to love a "good" child, or one she fancies resembles herself, and the other children in the family know it. The less-loved child may become naughty just to attract his mother's attention, or may prolong an illness because he enjoys his mother's loving care. Mothers will do well to remember that children want everything alike. As an example, one little girl tried hard to catch the measles (and succeeded) because her two brothers had measles and were getting all the attention. A mother should be fair in every way so that her children will not feel jealous and thwarted.

If there is one area in which American mothers generally can be criticized, it is their excessive emphasis on cleanliness. I recall three patients who exemplify this compulsive cleanliness: one, a ten-year-old boy, was the cleanest child on his street; another, a three-year-old girl, lived in dread of soiling her dresses; and the third child always washed her toys before playing with them. All three were the thoroughly wretched victims of their mothers' compulsion for cleanliness. They were my patients because they had developed serious psychiatric problems, and my first recommendation was that they be allowed to get dirty without fear of punishment. This freedom to get dirty is a privilege every child should have.

Mothers are right to insist that their children have a daily bath, a daily change of clothes, and help maintain a reasonably clean home. It cannot be denied that cleanliness is healthy; that tidiness is more comfortable than untidiness; and that good grooming is a badge of culture in our society. But to demand absolute cleanliness in children is abnormal and can result in serious maladjustment at the time and later on.

An overly fastidious mother creates an atmosphere of tension. She turns her home into a house of fear instead of one of happiness. To avoid tirades against leaving toys around, climbing on furniture, or tracking up the linoleum, her children prefer to play in the homes of their less-oppressed friends. When one little girl was playing in her yard with a neighbor's child who asked to go to the bathroom, she replied, "Let's go to your house. We might get ours dirty."

If you discover a tendency in yourself to harp on cleanliness, you might remember that play is instinctive in young children and is essential to their development. To be healthy mentally, children must be able to become totally absorbed in play. If they get dirty, they should not have to care or even be aware of it. You will help your child to enjoy play if you let him change into old clothes so that he can roll in the grass, climb, or enjoy other activities without worrying about whether they make him dirty or not.

Mothers should use similar good judgment regarding the care of the home. Boys and girls should be expected to keep their own rooms tidy and their clothes hung up, but a certain amount of disarray should be tolerated. Boys have a tendency to pile miscellaneous possessions in a heap on a table, and while it may look unsightly, they know what's there and don't want it disturbed. Girls often display programs, invitations and photographs on their mirrors. These may add nothing to the attractiveness of the room, but mothers should not object; the phase will pass.

Some mothers declare common rooms of the house—living room, dining room, even the kitchen—off limits to the children, so that the youngsters can only "mess up" their own rooms. This practice deprives a child of the chance to participate in family living. He should be allowed to use and share things with others, and should be permitted to keep something in these rooms so that he knows they are his rooms as well as his parents'.

The Father's Direction

The father-mother-child relationship is a shared relationship, a oneness of family. The father is more than a provider and top authority: he is most often the one who sits in judgment and metes out punishment. Unless he is unworthy of respect for some reason, he is an object of admiration to the preadolescent. Because he is seen far less than the mother, his commands get more respect. If he is wise, he will obtain obedience, not only because his children fear punishment and respect his superior strength, but also because they respect him with affection.

Several generations ago, the father's role in regard to his child's early development was considered of little importance. The mother was thought to be the most important factor, and it was she who was usually blamed if the youngster was abnormal or delinquent. At that time, the child's development was considered almost entirely from the physical viewpoint; when his physical life seemed excellent, he was termed healthy.

Now we recognize, however, that love and affection and "belonging"—the ingredients of security—are of immeasurable importance in forming the child's personality. And these must come not only from the mother, but equally from the father. Even during the first two or three months of the baby's life, when his interest is concentrated on eating and sleeping, the father can help in handling the child by changing diapers or giving him a bath. Dad can also play an important part in the following stages of development.

Why are fathers important?   A boy identifies himself with the dominant, strong figure in the household. Should this be his mother, he will probably fall in readily with her wishes and assume feminine attitudes. He may draw away from competitive sports and prefer quiet, domestic activities to the more active and boisterous ones of the typical child. Such submissive children are often considered as ideal youngsters because they cause no disturbance in the house. But their personalities are actually warped; in extreme cases they are unable to marry. Or if they marry, they prove unsatisfactory mates. They are the victims of "Mom-ism"—one of the major causes of insecurity in men today.

From earliest times, in our society, the father has been recognized as the head of the family. It was always he who made decisions and saw that they were carried out. The children gave him their utmost confidence because they believed in his unlimited strength and felt that their destiny was safe in his hands. He was believed to possess a true sense of values and a sense of humor; to be lively and high in his aims; to have time for his family. He tossed a ball or played horseshoes with his son, took him for hikes in the woods, or went fishing with him. He took his boy or girl on his knee and told tall tales, which the children loved. Many modern fathers are entirely different from the type described above.

A close relationship with the father helps greatly in the development of the preadolescent's personality at this most impressionable age. The youngster admires his father's strength and "know how." He dotes on his father's protection and if he knows dad is nearby, he may be reckless on an outing and show off. He recognizes his father's first place in the family and his male prerogatives. Father's chair is respected, though his choice of TV program is debated. If asked what he wants to be when he grows up, the child of this age might mention some colorful figure he knows or has seen on TV or has read about, but he also believes that all the qualities of these heroes are to be found in his father.

The preadolescent enjoys his dad's companionship—on hikes, fishing or camping trips, and swimming. He loves to putter with any kind of machinery or tools with his father. Such companionship promotes manliness in the boy; it counteracts the "sissiness" which may develop in a child tied to his mother's apron strings.

While fathers should take an active interest in their child's activities, it is not advisable to become involved personally in the youngster's disputes. A father should understand, for example, that if his child is hurt in a game, other children should not necessarily be blamed. Often one hears the story that Johnny started the fight and that Billy, merely trying to defend himself, was hurt. In this version, Johnny is the villain. Unless the evidence is overwhelming that Johnny is a persistent troublemaker, Billy's parents would be well advised to forget the incident; for where normal children are involved, Billy might start the fight tomorrow. If that happened, Billy's parents would be more than a little annoyed if their child were wrongly criticized throughout the neighborhood for hurting another.

In one community, the sons of two men friends became involved in a fight. The boys returned home, bruised and bloodied. Their parents went out into the street and continued the fight where the youngsters left off. A few days later, the boys were playing together again as though nothing had happened. But it was months before the fathers could talk to each other without embarrassment.

In a home where the child-parent relationship has provided a feeling of acceptance and security in love, the child will have a better chance of assuming an adequate place in the business world. If he feels sure of his parents' love, unworthy friendships or companions in his neighborhood and school will influence him little. He can refuse the dare to "follow the leader" if it means getting into trouble. Unlike the rejected boy, the boy who enjoys love and security at home doesn't need a gang to bolster up his feeling of adequacy. But a child handicapped by poor home life or parental neglect, and the resultant feeling of inadequacy, may respond to the influence of bad companions because they provide satisfactions no one else gives. In this case, his security comes from the combined strength of a gang whose members themselves are insecure.

The boy of this age is a hero worshipper. Therefore, if his father fails him because of unconcern about the family, or because he is too wrapped up in his business life and outside interests to spend much time at home, the boy will seek a father image to worship and imitate. The father thus loses a precious opportunity to build his child's personality and character. When he relegates all responsibility to the mother, just

as he metes out the weekly house allowance, he is being unfair to her, to his child, and to himself, for he robs himself of
the unequalled pleasures of fatherhood.

How the School Can Influence Personality

The child attending school for a full day spends more hours
with his teacher than with his parents. Therefore, the teacher
plays an important role in personality and character formation. An experienced teacher will be able to evaluate both the
personality of the child and his home training. Since each
child's background, training, and experience differ, the
teacher should make an accurate and fair judgment to determine the child's place in relation to the class as a whole. Then
she can direct him accordingly.

Not all teachers are ideal, any more than parents are. Not
all have the necessary temperament. For instance, Miss
Jennie was a hot-tempered disciplinarian, and Henry's mis-
chievousness often aroused her wrath. One day, when Henry
was passing a note from one girl to another, Miss Jennie saw
him and commanded him to bring it to her. Henry tore it
into bits instead. She demanded an apology, but he refused
to comply. Then she gave him a note to take home which
said he was a very disobedient boy. That night, when the
father heard the story, he held back his laughter and solemnly
told his boy always to stand by what he felt sure was right,
even though someone else might think it wrong. "Let's forget it," he said, "and if Miss Jennie asks you anything, just
say your father took care of it." The father's attitude seems
more reasonable than Miss Jennie's.

The child who is well adjusted at home will most likely
cooperate with the teacher and respect her rules. Unless she
does something to offend him, such as rebuking him before
the class for a trivial offense, the youngster will like the
teacher and will be liked in return.

It also follows that the child who has difficulty at home
will have difficulties at school. A teacher can generally win
him over to acceptance of the rules if she is patient and kind,
praising him when praise is deserved, chiding him when he

disturbs the peace or refuses to cooperate, even meting out some punishment when needed, but always with consideration of his pride and feelings. She should overlook little faults of such a child but make it plain that she will not tolerate major transgressions.

Parents can often make up for the defects of teachers. For instance, most teachers hope to be impartial. But it isn't long before keen little preadolescents become aware that certain children are praised and favored, while others evidently annoy the teacher and are scolded and disciplined often. Every child wants approval and praise; he has his pride and a certain dignity to maintain. If he is ridiculed or made to feel small in front of his classmates, he will be bitterly hurt. His parents should strive to reassure him of his worth and give him the encouragement denied him by the teacher.

Some teachers devise cruel ways of hurting a child's pride. Such methods may bring obedience through fear, but they can also bring hatred. A poor speller was held up to ridicule by his fourth-grade teacher whenever he missed a word. The youngster grew to hate spelling and never learned to spell properly. Results might have been different if the child's mother, recognizing the teacher's defects, had helped with the spelling lessons.

The teacher who is impatient with a poor reader, not only fails to improve the child's reading, but makes him unwilling to read. Since reading is essential to success in any field, the teacher is thus serving to handicap the youngster for life. Parents should realize that the cause of reading difficulty may be physical, such as poor vision, or emotional. If you find that your child is not improving his reading ability, perhaps because the teacher hasn't time to teach properly, you should try to secure special help for him. This must be done before he reaches adolescence. Too often such a child is allowed to drift along until his schooling is almost completed.

There are a few teachers who are such strict disciplinarians that they frighten pupils into abject submission and cause the more sensitive ones to develop symptoms of excessive nervousness. If a teacher terrifies your child, you should discuss the problem with school authorities.

The solicitous teacher chooses her profession because of a liking for children and a pride in teaching them. Education by such a teacher is not limited to cramming facts into young minds, preparing them to pass the grade at the end of the year. It also has as one of its primary functions the development of the child into a wholesome, socially adjusted individual.

Since most children are eager for the teacher's praise, they will object if certain children are specially favored. A teacher's pet is quickly identified, long before the teacher herself recognizes her preference. This favored child may show a special capability in his studies, may be well-behaved and cooperative, or may deliberately ingratiate himself to win approval. Usually the "pets" are heartily disliked: the other children seek revenge, usually outside of the classroom, but occasionally they laugh at them in school, or trip them as they pass by. A biased teacher may loudly scold the naughty child and not seek the reason for the evident dislike expressed for the good little pupil. Sometimes the "pets" do not want the preference shown them and deliberately are mischievous to prove that they are no different from the others. As a parent, you should understand that this is a common reaction.

A preadolescent child repeatedly hurt by rebuke may refuse to go to school, saying he hates the teacher. Interference by a parent, which is ordinarily unwise in many cases of childish complaints, is then necessary. A quiet talk may help both teacher and parent understand the difficulty, and may enable them to work together to make the child happier and more cooperative.

Sometimes truancy can be traced to a teacher's perfectionism. Since failures reflect upon her teaching ability, having her pupils pass may become her sole objective. Parents sometimes err in the same way by urging a child beyond his intellectual powers, making him nervous and sometimes stubborn. The preadolescent who can't keep up with the standards his parents set may feel no urge to do better; he may actively dislike school and play hooky. Punishment for this misconduct may deter him from repeating this offense if his bitterness is not too great. However, his dislike for school may be so intense that truancy becomes chronic. If parents are unable to overcome this fault through love and admonition, and the school psychologist is unsuccessful in finding the cause and remedy, psychiatric help may be needed to prevent development of delinquency. The case is not hopeless in a child of this age. Children do not stay out of school simply because of the call of the great outdoors; they would much rather attend school, where they can find companionship with their age mates.

A child's personality can also be permanently warped if a teacher continually overemphasizes the superior intelligence of a few "stars" in the class. A parent's demand that a child have as good grades as another child in the family or neighborhood can be equally scarring. Betty was continually prodded by her mother to keep up with her unusually bright cousin. Betty was an entirely normal child, but her mother's insistence that she keep pace with a superior student made her so self-conscious and discouraged that she was continually shaken and she failed to do her best. She never lost her feeling of inferiority. She had an upset stomach before any test and was a nervous wreck after every examination. Whenever she faced any competition as an adult, she was continually fearful of failure.

Singling out children for special attention sometimes leaves its mark on the favored one, too. Not long ago, I treated an outstanding, intellectually gifted physicist, who had made no friends in elementary or high school. All teachers promoted him in every way possible; for example, whenever the teachers wanted to show off their class to visitors, he was the only one who was asked questions. He was the champion "quiz kid" and received all the honors. The other children disliked him and refused to associate with him, especially since he was poor in sports. He developed fear and anxiety and ultimately needed a psychiatrist's care, while his less gifted—but normally adjusted—classmates became happy adults.

In a world that needs mutual cooperation and understanding, fostering the highly competitive, individualistic spirit in a child adds little to his social and cultural development. Moreover, the competitive grading system of our modern schools aids neither the very bright nor the dull. It only provides the teacher with a means of domination. There is the possibility that the bright child who receives excellent grades fears, even hates, any competitor who threatens his top position.

For those who are slow in school subjects, the marking system may so discourage them that they lose their desire to learn. They feel debased and unhappy. They develop, not only a distaste for school, but also lack self-confidence and responsibility.

Children who are thus made to feel unhappy in school will think of truancy as a last resort. They will first express their unhappiness by naughty deeds, such as whispering or talking out loud, shooting spit balls at other children, dropping books and pencils to make noise, or refusing to study. A teacher with such a youngster in her charge should ask herself what has upset him. She has no right to assume that he is merely spoiled, that he is dull, or that he is incurably bad, unless special tests have contributed to these opinions. This child, without careful direction, may tend toward delinquency—and delinquency can be prevented at this stage during which a child is most easily influenced.

If a teacher's load is too heavy and she cannot give individual attention to a little rebel, she should confer with the parent and encourage him to try to establish a better relationship with the child. Praise and awards of special privileges at home for the child's better conduct and higher marks will provide encouragement; scolding and punishment may bring rebellion and utter discouragement.

It will often be found that poor homework and therefore poor progress in school are due to distractions at home, such as having no quiet place in which to study, an intrusive radio or television set, too many visitors in the home, or too little rest. Occasionally, a listless child who shows disinterest in his studies, who refuses to respond to urging and to scolding, may not be lazy or stupid, as the teacher might suspect. He may be listless because he is undernourished. The school doctor or nurse may suggest a more suitable diet for him.

In most grades, there is at least one youngster who is a disturbing element, not because he is unintelligent or maladjusted, but because he is extra bright and not kept busy. Because he need study very little, he may become mischievous in order to occupy his mind. Such a child should be given extra assignments and should do all his studying in school, if possible. If he tends to show off in class recitations, the teacher will do well to ignore him until other children have had their chance.

Some children appear to teem with energy and have difficulty keeping still. The wise teacher recognizes this. Philip was an eager, willing child, but extremely hyperactive. The teacher tried to keep him busy doing errands, erasing the board, or putting assignments on the board. One day, when a supervisor was visiting the room, the teacher quietly called attention to Philip. He had tied a rope beneath his desk and was swinging his feet on it; he was intently studying the book in his left hand and waving a ruler to and fro in his right hand, all the while chewing gum at a furious rate. "I pretend not to notice," the teacher explained. "Philip is actually studying hard."

Playmates, Playthings, and Personality

Home surroundings, playmates and neighborhood all contribute to your child's personality. The ordinary youngster accepts his home and neighborhood and makes few comparisons. He may prefer someone else's yard because it has a tree or fence to climb, or an old building that can be used as a clubhouse. Most youngsters' play is wholesome and constructive. If, however, your child engages in activities that are socially undesirable, try to substitute wholesome play instead. Little girls "playing funeral" or "having a baby" will just as easily respond to laundering doll clothes, or cooking something they themselves can eat, or having a tea party of milk and cookies. If provided the materials, young boys will keep store, or build something, instead of pretending holdups, swimming in forbidden waters, or destroying property.

Playmates teach a child that he is not all-important, that he must give and take in order to get along with people, that he must play fair—or perhaps get pummelled. The boy learns the value of self-defense; he also learns how to accept unavoidable defeat.

Companions can also exert an evil influence. Through bad companionship a child learns to lie, swear and steal; he may even drift into crime. If for any reason he does not receive at home the full measure of love and protection he needs for proper nurture, he may escape into the folds of a gang whose mannerisms and daring he imitates. It is therefore important that your children feel free to bring their friends home and entertain them. This freedom will help your child feel at home with you in his social relationships. He will accept the fact that you should meet and know his friends, and he will feel comfortable about carrying on normal activities with your knowledge and consent. To follow this policy means that you must give up ideas of maintaining a spotless home. But on the other hand, you may be surprised at how clean your home can be when your youngsters are permitted to entertain and are given some responsibility for keeping up appearances.

It is a good idea, wherever possible, to give your boy a dog at this time. A boy needs to give and receive love, and when his parents do not give him their affection and understanding, he needs to tell his troubles to somebody; a dog often serves as confidant.

Caring for a puppy and raising him to be a good dog involves chores that develop a boy's sense of responsibility. It should be his duty to housebreak the pup and feed him, and to clean up the dirt and litter he makes. He should train his dog in acceptable conduct and good manners. Just as the boy must be taught to behave properly, so the boy will train his dog, not with harsh words and beatings, but with firm directions, calm and moderate punishment, and rewarding praise. The lad who is responsible for his dog's health and good manners learns a lesson about the value of proper living and good behavior for himself. He comes to understand that there is justice in punishment for breaking established rules—and that it is foolhardy to break the rules.

Kindness, loyalty and control of the temper and the will are no more born in a boy than in a dog. They are acquired only through instruction and discipline, a practical truth your child can learn when he applies this reasoning to his dog.

Developing Religious Beliefs

A belief in the power of God—His watch over children, His protection, His awareness of their transgressions and His forgiveness, His willingness to answer their prayers—can best be fostered at this age. Such a belief helps immeasurably in the teen years just around the corner. Even parents who have drifted away from their church usually want their children to learn and follow its teachings as a guidance to good conduct. Some parents, indifferent to all faiths, nevertheless want their youngsters trained in the study of the Bible as literature so that they will not be ignorant of that classic in later years.

The preadolescent child listens to Bible stories with the same interest he earlier gave to fairy tales. He learns that whereas fairy tales are pure phantasy and are designed for entertainment, the miraculous Bible stories are true because they came from God. At this pliant age, he readily accepts these teachings.

He should regard God as a kindly Father who listens to his prayers. Thus, the additions he makes to his bedside prayers are very personal and often astonishing. For example, a seven-year-old girl grew tired of her elders' many requests to go upstairs and get this or that, take this to the neighbor, or run to the store. At night she secretly asked God to make her doll alive so that it could help with her chores.

The school child should believe, not only in God's goodness, but also in His demand for goodness in the child. This can be a strong factor in the development of acceptable behavior. The school boy doesn't pull his sister's hair at home, because his mother would punish him; but he has no compunctions against yanking it when his mother is not present. He may believe that there is nothing wrong about this; it's just one of those things mother doesn't like. But he has great compunctions about taking money from her pocketbook, not because he will be punished at home or by the law, but because God sees him. Through his religious training, the child thus attains, not only a respect for parental approval and a respect for inflexible laws, but also a desire for God's approval.

Three boys found a purse in a gutter. One suggested that they divide the money. Lennie demurred. "Come on," one boy said, "nobody will see us." Lennie stood firm. "God sees us," he answered. The others jeered but were uncomfortable. "Well then, let's take it to the police station and get a reward," one suggested. This made them feel important and off they ran. The knowledge that there was no way to hide from God served as a deterrent to wrongdoing.

The idea of regular church attendance is easily accepted at this time. It becomes a duty and a habit that often continues throughout life. Sometimes it is thrown off in adult years, sometimes even a belief in the Almighty is discarded, but a faith well-grounded in these formative years is rarely entirely lost.

When your child is at this age of dawning social and moral responsibility, therefore, you should strive to lay the foundation for his well-balanced personality at home, at school, and at church, using the pressure of social codes as a guide. The child cannot walk alone; he must have guidance. This does not mean that a youngster whose training is neglected at this period always turns out "bad." Many factors determine his personality, and not all exert their influence at the same time. But precepts instilled in this preadolescent period will never be entirely lost, whatever influences and experiences later tend to mar or distort the individual character.

CHAPTER SIX

Personality Adjustment of Adolescence

Adolescence is a truly critical period in your child's life. It is a time of stepping up and out. Now almost adult, the youngster casts off old childish ways and acquires new patterns of behavior which befit grown-ups. In this period your child not only grows to adult stature but also prepares for vast responsibilities which adults are called upon to assume. He must make many adjustments so that he can fit adequately and happily into the larger social family. As he chips his way out of the protecting shell of parental control, he is often unaware of what is happening. He doesn't know where he is going, but he is all steamed up about getting there. And he doesn't want anyone to get in his way.

This is a wonderful time of life if the adolescent has been prepared for his new experiences by a careful shaping of his personality in his earlier years. If his training has been neglected, he may be fearful of each new step in his development, for he must battle his way through storms which beat heavily against the unprepared. He may emerge victorious or he may be unable to face and conquer his adolescent problems, whereupon society may reject him.

The Changes at Puberty

At the onset of puberty, when your child acquires sexual characteristics, even though he be the mildest, most obedient youngster, he may shock you by suddenly "acting up." If you say chidingly, "This isn't our little boy!" he will probably be disturbed. He doesn't feel like a little boy. He is a young man, and why can't you see it?

The increasing activity of his glands at puberty releases tremendous energy, which he works off in part by throwing himself into sports. These games promote health and increase strength, agility, and gracefulness. However, his bursts of speed and enthusiasm do not last indefinitely, and he alternates between a seemingly tireless energy and an utter slump. He may have to be pulled out of bed so that he will get to school in time; yet that same night he may stay out very late and fall asleep immediately upon climbing into bed. It might take a fire alarm to arouse him the next morning. Then he is up and out again.

Often the fatigued adolescent is accused of laziness. He is goaded by his elders to activity when he really should be resting. On the other hand, an oversympathetic mother may worry too much over his tiredness and tell him to forget his books and go to bed. This is unwarranted; if play interferes with study, play, not studies, should be limited. Proper hours of sleep and rest will restore his washed-out pep, but time lost from study is difficult to make up.

The change in body structure at puberty which so clearly differentiates the sexual aspects of boys and girls also produces differences in strength and motor development. A boy's strength normally doubles between the ages of twelve and sixteen, after which time it may gradually decrease. The degree of his ultimate strength will depend largely upon how active he is in young manhood and what demands are made upon his strength. A girl increases in strength up to the age of thirteen or fourteen. There is a considerable decrease in the rate of growth of her muscular powers after that, unless she is athletically inclined and engages in sports. However, even the very active girl cannot have the strength of the normal boy. Special feats she exhibits are due to skills she has learned, not to superior strength. In addition to the difference in muscular strength between the sexes, the boy develops a deeper chest, which enables him to breathe more deeply. He also has an increased systolic blood pressure when his work load is increased.

The adolescent boy's motor ability builds up his self-esteem. He says, "Here, feel my muscle." He begins to feel competent in coping with problems in his environment and the challenges of his age group. The girl's motor skill declines, not only because she lacks the physique, but also because social edicts against tomboyishness forbid her from developing them. She delights in working off energy by dancing fast and furiously. She attends all the games, not to participate, but to yell.

Puberty brings abrupt physiological changes, which mature the body and its organs in preparation for reproduction. But God's law imposes a need for sex control among the young; unlike animals, they cannot be uninhibited and promiscuous. The conflict between the adolescent's strange new drive and the need to control it bewilders him. He does not know the causes of the inner tensions that result in his emotional instability.

Puberty usually starts in girls during the eleventh or twelfth year, and in boys one or two years later. The physical changes are brought about by the increasing activity of the endocrine glands, which secrete hormones into the system, and soon this activity results in the formation of spermatozoa and ova, all ready for the reproduction of a new life. In most individuals the ability to procreate does not come until a few years after puberty begins, but sometimes newspapers report a baby born to a pre-teen-age girl.

Primary sex changes indicate the rate of maturation. Menstruation begins in the girl. It may come with irregularity at first and be attended with some pain and nervousness. Unless she has been told about this subject, she may be bewildered and shocked and run to her mother in alarm. A thoughtful mother will already have explained that this procedure occurs every month and that it is the period when the uterus prepares for reception of a fertilized ovum, or egg. When no ovum is formed after a short time, the thickened lining of the uterus sluffs off, causing bleeding. The girl should be assured that this hemorrhage lasts only a few days and is in no way dangerous. She should be taught the hygienic measures which will keep her sweet and clean.

Some mothers explain menstruation as the monthly curse of all women. They warn the terrified daughter that she must never mention to anyone that she is "unwell." In this way, the girl may come to regard menstruation as a shaming, detestable function, a sickness she must endure because of her sex. Since physical symptoms such as abdominal cramps, nausea, headache, and backache often precede or attend the first few menstruations, the wrongly informed girl will expect them every time. Pain and distress that attend the period will be magnified in her sensitive nervous system. If these symptoms persist, she may require a physician's care, for unless she obtains proper medication and instruction, her suffering may become chronic.

The boy's direct evidence of his maturity as a procreator is the occurrence of occasional nightly emissions, which result when hormones overcharge the enlarging sex glands. He too must be assured that this is a normal occurrence and in no way reflects upon his moral integrity. If this is not explained to him, some other boy no wiser than he, or some advertisement he reads may cause him to believe that he has a venereal disease or has injured himself by masturbation. Not all mothers understand the meaning of this phenomenon. They may have false ideas regarding it and may torture him with reproaches and insinuations.

Secondary sex characteristics are also quite evident in both sexes. The girl's breasts enlarge rapidly and become tender. Dismayed by their protrusion, she may try to hide them by wearing a tight binder, an unhealthy practice which her mother should warn her against. Most modern girls, however, go to the opposite extreme. By the time they reach adolescence, they have become exposed to innumerable advertisements and pictures showing entertainers whose main characteristic is the size of their busts. The girl whose bosom develops slowly may feel that she is not a complete female. She may wear falsies to pretend a size she thinks attractive.

A noticeable secondary characteristic of the maturing process in both girls and boys is a change from the silky hair of childhood to the heavier hair of adulthood. The hair gradually darkens to the shade it will retain until it turns gray. Hair appears in the pubic areas, on the arms and legs, and in the armpits. The boy acquires hair on his chest and face, a sign he anxiously awaits as proof of his manhood.

The sweat glands also enlarge and become increasingly active. The odor disturbs the adolescent boy and girl and they daub on cheap and strong-smelling perfumes or lotions. The male usually soon gives up the habit, except perhaps for mild shave lotions. Girls continue to like perfumes but use them more delicately.

You should teach your adolescents that only cleanliness controls body odors and that when perfume is mixed with body odor it may be more obnoxious than the body odor alone. When in spite of frequent baths the adolescent continues to suffer from a body odor, you would do well to seek out the cause. Sometimes such odors are due to certain foods.

Skin troubles are also common at this age. As the once delicate skin thickens and coarsens at puberty, the pores enlarge and pimples sometimes develop, whereupon boys and girls may try various lotions and salves they see advertised. They should instead seek the care and advice of a physician. He may recommend the use of a bland soap and water instead of fancy-named facial creams, and also reassure the youngster that the skin disorder will soon disappear.

The male adolescent is embarrassed by the breaking of his voice at what he considers to be the most annoying times. His beautiful choir-boy soprano deserts him and his voice squeaks, but tomorrow he will be a tenor or baritone. He should be told that this disturbance is the result of his expanding voice box. Boys love to sing loudly and yell at the top of their voices during games; they should be warned at this time of the strain on their developing voices.

Other bodily changes are more pleasing. As his limbs lengthen, the boy's shoulders broaden, his chest deepens, and the baby fat around the body disappears. The girl's form changes from a bean-pole shape to pleasing curves and broadened hips. Former round baby faces lengthen, the lips become fuller, and the bone structure becomes more apparent; the head, which had grown faster than the rest of the body, now becomes of proportionate size.

Changes in height are rapid at this stage. The boy wants

to grow tall fast; he doesn't want to be a sawed-off runt. The girl, however, becomes anxious if she is taller than her girl friends or the boys she knows. She is embarrassed by her long limbs; she thinks large-sized gloves and shoes are simply awful. She knows that most men do not like women taller than themselves and is afraid that she will be an old maid. She should be assured that girls who are tall often stop growing early and may even turn out to be of average height, that physical growth varies so greatly in different persons that early tallness and shortness can be deceiving.

The youngster who is taller or shorter than normal may develop serious psychological problems. For instance, an over-sized youngster is often expected to act his size rather than his age. "You big clown," a father growls at his boy, "brace up and be a man." But when the boy does act like a man by staying out late, he is told that he is actually a very young boy. This only serves to confuse the youngster. Chores at home are often assigned according to his size, regardless of his true age and strength. His mother's statement, "You are big enough now to help around the place," may be true. But because he may eat like a horse is no reason for expecting this young colt to carry a horse's load.

Teen-age boys like to excel in sports; it makes them feel manly. Unfortunately, size is a great asset in many games. The short adolescent should enter sports like tennis and swimming, where height is not such a great advantage. Knowing that he excels in one sport allows him to sit contentedly on the sidelines and root for his school football or basketball team.

Unless the short boy conquers his inferiority feeling, he may grow up to be a very disagreeable person. He may show cockiness in his strutting walk, try to dominate his associates, or be boastful and argumentative. The short person who develops a sense of humor and doesn't resent wisecracks about his height can attain an admirable status of manhood, where his lack of height goes unnoted because of his friendly personality.

While an adolescent boy can laugh over his excessive weight, a girl is badly hurt when she is called fat. She will usually outgrow her obesity, but in some cases, especially where the parents are heavy eaters, she may never gain control over her appetite and may fight obesity for the rest of her life.

Adolescence is often called the awkward age, but this awkwardness is not due to puberty itself. In part, the ungainliness is due to the unaccustomed length of limbs. More especially, the child seems ungainly because he outgrows clothes which cannot be replaced fast enough to prevent sleeves and pant legs from being embarrassingly short. Even the adolescent's new clothes, which fit perfectly, may make him look awkward. He usually has disdain for the clothes of the preadolescent and wants grown-up clothes. He selects garments that are usually cheap, of crude cut and poor material, and often in poor taste. They may be loud and vulgar, but if that is what the crowd is wearing, that is what he wants to have. Girls know that shorts and slacks and shabby shoes add nothing to their scrawny looks, but they refuse to be different from other girls.

The adolescent boy finds the adjustment to social requirements much to his distaste. He is reluctant to conform, and when he finally gives in he has difficulty in acquiring the social graces. He is self-conscious and awkward.

Homely features usually make a girl very self-conscious and gawky. Since the nose lengthens out of proportion to her other features at first, the big-nosed girl may become very unhappy, especially if it is badly shaped. Parents are conscious of the need for beautiful teeth and will have their daughter wear dental braces for years if necessary. They rarely consider altering an ugly nose; yet a girl's whole personality can be warped by her distress over a misshapen nose.

Growing up to the size, shape and strength of adulthood is only one phase of adolescence. Psychological growth—being able and willing to accept the responsibilities of adulthood—is a more important process. Before your adolescent can adjust to the demands of an exacting society and prepare himself for happy living with others, he must learn that he cannot expect to obtain everything he desires, nor even all that he may need; and that he cannot push on toward manhood thinking only of himself and his own advancement. He must learn to give as well as take, to control his emotions, to smile when he feels like scowling, to accept disappointments and frustrations without rebellion or bitterness. This is not easy. The glandular activity which is altering his physical being creates an inner pressure which causes increased emotional excitability. How he controls and alters these emotions, how well he bears the storms and stresses that come, determine the kind of adult he will be.

Psychological Changes of Adolescence

The adolescent feels that he is no longer a child and therefore thinks he should be treated like a grown-up. He wants to be recognized as an individual with certain rights, with opinions to be listened to and respected. He has very positive opinions on most subjects and resents having them laughed at or brushed off. He changes his opinion many times, but does not want to be reminded of this, and opposition to any of his ideas may cause him to retain them.

He causes his parents great concern, and they also bother him. They demand that he act like a man, not a little boy; yet, when he asserts himself like a man, he is sharply rebuked and put in his place. He is reminded that his parents still hold authority, that they know what is best for him and will stand for none of his nonsense. This hurts his self-esteem. No wonder the adolescent is sometimes called the "marginal man," one who no longer belongs to the childish group into which he once fitted so well, nor is yet accepted by the privileged group to which he now aspires.

Your adolescent's struggle for independence should be recognized as a normal sign of his maturing process. How can he learn to fly if he is not allowed to try his wings? He cannot know his strength until he tries it out. He needs to experiment and profit from his failures.

He soon discovers a surprisingly different world. If his parents try to tell him what to expect from life, he often does not want, even resents, their interference. He cannot be protected from every danger and frustration, nor should he be.

Yet despite his apparent self-confidence, he does not want to cast off your parental protection. When baffled by his problems and when he no longer can endure the frustrations which arise from his lack of experience, he wants to feel assured that he can continue to lean on you as he has in the past. If he wants your help, he will probably ask for it expectantly and confidently; however, he does not want advice thrust upon him. Often he would rather do something wrong and pay for his mistake than be shown how to do it properly. Everyone has a right to make mistakes—and this is one right the adolescent fully insists upon!

Your teen-ager is a very busy person. He is primarily intent upon having a good time, but will manage to keep up his studies well enough to get by if he needs good grades to remain on a team or qualify for college. He may want to attend college chiefly to acquire culture; more often he is interested in obtaining the education required for the kind of job he wants; or, he may simply have social aspirations to be a college graduate. Usually his idea of what kind of vocation he should pursue vacillates as he meets or learns of adults with attractive positions in the business, commercial, professional, or political world. Those adolescents with lesser ambitions aim to get through high school as soon as possible and find a good-paying job.

The girl, through natural desire and the inspiration of her parents, looks forward to marriage. In her mind, marriage should be financially attractive if possible, but most of all she wants to marry for love. She will laugh in derision if anyone tries to repeat the old saw that there is a "lid for every pot;" she knows that there are too many unmarried women and that she cannot simply wait passively for marriage. But unless she knows she is quite unattractive, she has high hopes. For this reason an adolescent girl may be content to get through school and obtain a job that will support her until she finds a husband. If the job brings her into contact with eligible males, so much the better. However, a girl may also look forward to a job that will pay well and at the same time bring social recognition. She may want to go to college to prepare for some profession, or gain social prestige, or in hopes that she will find a husband. These various considerations influence the quality of scholarship that adolescents display in high school.

For most youngsters, adolescence is the most selfish time of life besides infancy. The adolescent has an inflated opinion of himself; he thinks that he is just as good as anyone else, and probably a bit better than many people he knows. He may become very angry at anyone who belittles his ego. If he feels unappreciated, his distress can lead to a serious maladjustment of personality.

A number of teen-age girls were having a party. Marie was having a lot of fun, but she noticed Lillian sulking in a corner. She tried to coax her into the games. Lillian said sneeringly, "Those girls make me sick. I'm just as good as they are, but they ignore me." Marie replied, "They wouldn't notice me either if I sat back here alone; I get right in the middle and have fun." The truth was that Lillian didn't think herself as good as the others. Her father was unable to support his large family and they were partly on relief, and Lillian felt debased by the way she had to live. She felt that she had been denied the opportunity to prove that she was just as good as anyone else. Thus, her antisocial attitudes were caused directly by the harm done to her ego.

Your adolescent cares very little about anything but his own development and advancement. However hurt you may feel about this apparent selfishness, you should recognize it as quite normal. He soon will assume the responsibilities of adulthood and now he must concentrate upon attaining that status to the exclusion of other things. Two factors contribute to his selfishness: he has a teeming energy, which he expends in new interests; he senses that never again will he have as many opportunities for a good time.

An adolescent's enjoyments usually are those of the crowd, such as dances, parties, outings. Movies, theatre, television, or reading may be the pleasure of the moment; the teen-ager wants to enjoy it with someone else of his own age. He prefers either a pal "to bat around with" or a clique composed of friends of his own age, who have similar interests, codes, and beliefs and who show him the respect his elders deny him.

His group displays little of the ritualistic loyalty that existed in the early gang of the ten-year-olds. He pretends a preference for his own crowd, but if he gets a chance to join a clique of a higher order, which he admires, he abruptly changes to the new group. He wants the same kind of clothes, the same amount of spending money, the same privileges outside home that others of his group have. If he lacks certain social qualifications, he may try to make up for it by excelling in athletics, or working to get elected to office in school.

A teen-age girl becomes socially conscious in school if her parents have not trained her in this area earlier. She pals with one or two girls. Together they are a part of a larger group which parties together. The two girls exchange secrets, reveal and relieve their frustrations, share their dreams and aspirations; they believe that no one else understands or accepts them without criticism. Girl chums conduct long telephone conversations almost every night, even though they have parted only an hour or two before. The giggling talk is often about boys, and is conducted largely in a gobbledegook language which parents aren't supposed to understand. Parents often get annoyed with this prolonged duet and demand an end to the silliness; they either want the phone, expect a call, or just can't stand that nonsense any longer. The chums are disgusted at the selfishness of the old folks.

Adolescents regard their peers' opinions much more highly than those of their parents. As they gain confidence in their own judgments, they begin to look critically at their parents, who a few years before were quite infallible. A mother is asked, "Must you wear that old dress?" Father is asked why he doesn't buy a decent-looking car. And why can't they paint the house and get some decent furniture? The hurt parent thinks the teen-ager is getting too big for his breeches. Yet this behavior in the adolescent is entirely normal. As he raises his sights, he wants to be proud of his parents and his home. His complaining is similar to that which his parents did earlier when they wanted him to be a credit to themselves.

It may be, however, that the parents have already stretched their budget to provide their children with comforts and pleasures their friends enjoy. Doctor bills, repair bills, or a lowered income may have brought financial difficulties. Parents naturally want to spare their children financial worries, but if children compare their parents and home unfavorably with other parents and homes, they should be told frankly about family finances. Their cooperation can usually be obtained if they are taken into the parents' confidence. But the children must feel they are being told the truth, not just being held off with excuses.

In homes where a happy relationship exists between parent and child, the child may take a job after school hours to help the family budget. This should be his own idea, though it may be tactfully suggested. It should not be demanded of him, if he is to feel his manliness and loyalty in sharing family troubles. Some parents continually tell their child how much they have done for him and emphasize his ungratefulness. His resentfulness is mixed with a feeling of guilt. He likes to believe that everything his parents have done for him was his right, that nothing they did was begrudged.

Part of the child's disillusionment regarding his parents is due to the fact that these adults often fail to understand the problems of growing up. They war against "indecent" clothes, especially strapless dresses and skimpy bathing suits; against youngsters trooping off for hot dogs after a dance which brings them home very late; and against many other fads of today's youngsters. Usually they fear that their children will drink to excess, break traffic laws, or give way to sex temptations. *Bluntly, they do not trust their children.*

Even children who have had proper training and have attained a high moral sense resent this distrusting attitude of parents. They feel entirely able to take care of themselves. They come to believe that their parents object to everything that is new and different and are old-fashioned and narrow. The adolescent who has not been well trained earlier can still be properly influenced at this stage, for he is highly impressionable and emotional. But threats of punishment, deprivation of privileges, or keeping close watch over his activities (which he scorns as spying) will hardly be effective now. Unless the break between parent and child is severe, the love between them and the teen-ager's sense of loyalty may awaken him to the problems he is facing.

Sometimes parents find it difficult to trust their children fully. However, a certain measure of supervision on the part of parents is necessary in view of modern conditions. Parents must sometimes take a firm stand against real moral dangers into which their adolescent children may fall if not emphatically warned and directed.

Corporal punishment for an adolescent often hurts his self-esteem, and, as we stressed earlier, his ego is most important to him. The discipline usually effective at this age is an appeal to the child's reason, his moral sense, and his idea of fairness. A frank discussion of the offense and its dangers to the youngster will not be soon forgotten, nor will it bring resentment and rebellion.

Teen-age boys and girls love to bring friends into the home. The mother should not chance disgracing the child by disregarding her own appearance. A father who shames his youngster by sprawling in his chair with shirt and shoes off is not playing fair. He may need rest and relaxation, but he should know his child wants him to compare favorably with the fathers of his friends. Unless the teen-ager can entertain his pals at home, he will enjoy their company elsewhere, even if it has to be a pool room, or other undesirable environment.

However, your children do not want you around when they have company. They no longer want you to attend movies with them, except on special occasions. They may become angry if you call for them at parties. They do not want you listening in on their phone conversations, however unimportant their chatter.

A fifteen-year-old girl gave a large party. Her mother greeted the guests when they arrived and then sat in the next room, reading a book. Suddenly she got up and closed the door, whereupon the girl opened it and asked her mother if they were being too noisy. "Oh no," the mother replied, "I was afraid your friends could see me and would think they had to be quiet. I don't want to spoil their good time." Not all parents are so understanding.

Teen-agers may sometimes criticize their parents, often

scorn their opinions, and are even sassy. They nevertheless crave their parents' approval and interest—*when it is not obtrusive*. Sometimes the adolescent will confide at length and bare his soul to a sympathetic parent. On other occasions he will shut up when questioned about his aspirations and plans; now he regards them as strictly his own private business. This inconsistent blowing of hot and cold results from his efforts to work out his problems and conflicts by himself. It is well to remember that when he volunteers his confidence, he probably isn't seeking advice. Actually he wants approval. And usually he wants sympathy, not criticism.

Long before adolescence, the child should begin to assume certain duties at home. The adolescent girl should take care of her own room and do some of her own mending; except in exceptional cases, she should not be required to do the family mending. She should also help with the dishes. The boy may willingly cut the grass or wash the car, and even whistle while he works, provided he is allowed a certain leeway in selecting the time when the duty must be performed. To require him to do his chores when he is to play on the team, or has a date, will bring a fierce rebellion. Remember how you would have acted under the same circumstances!

A chore well done should be given simple appreciative approval. Don't say a flattering compliment in hopes that the job will be done without protest next time. Teen-agers can, with extraordinary sharpness, detect motives. And don't criticize minor mistakes; too much carping will bring distaste for the job.

A fourteen-year-old girl watched her mother making an apple pie and decided to make one herself. Her mother gave her some dough, a small pie plate, and told her to go ahead. That evening the girl proudly set her pie before her father. She watched his face for an expression of pleasure. He said, "Not bad, if you hadn't forgotten the sugar." Humbled, she did not attempt pie making again for a long time. Had her father said, "I'd like it a little sweeter," or remarked to the mother, "Some day that girl will be a fine cook like you," the girl would have been encouraged to keep baking pies and doubtless would have done better the next time.

Except in families struggling to keep within a budget, it is generally conceded that adolescent children should have an allowance. How much that allowance should be depends, of course, upon what the youngster is supposed to buy with it. He may be allowed to buy certain daytime clothes—a proudful privilege to most children. The selection may be outrageous according to parental taste, but it may be just what other teen-agers are wearing, and therefore most desirable to the child. Usually, the allowance is merely spending money to be used at soda fountains and movie houses. If the amount is too small, or the child's tastes too expensive, borrowing on the next installment is frequent. Thus begins a bad habit of spending beyond one's resources. If reasonably possible, the allowance should be equal to that which his friends receive. He should be trained to make the allowance reach; one week of over-spending should mean self-deprivation next week.

Whether children should be paid for doing chores at home is a much-debated question. Being paid may make the task more acceptable, but it does not always encourage responsibility for doing one's part as a member of the family. Rewarding by praise, by unexpected occasional gifts, or by special privileges, may be a better practice.

You should gradually increase the allowance as the child grows and provided his school work does not fall behind. But you should also encourage him to earn money of his own, for a hard-earned dollar is more wisely spent than one unearned. The boy with a paper route accepts a responsibility as heavy as any he will meet later in life: the obligation to work when he would rather be at home; the requirement that he never fail in deliveries; the demand that he collect the bill and keep records; the realization that a job contracted for must be faithfully performed—all these things help build character. Unless the family is poor and the boy is working to help support the family, he should be allowed to spend his earned money any way he pleases. However, he should be taught the value of spending it wisely for needed articles, or for special things he wants which his family cannot or will not provide. For example, a radio for his own room may be an especially proud possession if he earned it himself.

Girls have few ways of earning money. Their most popular source of income is baby sitting. This pays well but must be carefully regulated. If your daughter is to become a sitter, you should be well-informed about the families who hire her, what her responsibilities are, and whether she will be brought home at the conclusion of her job. She must know how to reach the parents of the child she is guarding, and you should also be available by phone. She should be instructed as to what to do in case of accidents which may occur, and also how to prevent them. She should never be allowed to baby sit with problem children. Most of all, she should be mature enough to realize her responsibilities and able to defend her charges and herself. Baby sitting by very young teen-agers should not be allowed.

Emotional Changes of Adolescence

In many instances the emotional excesses of adolescents should be tolerated or ignored; if uncontrolled, they should be rebuked. A teen-ager ordinarily craves approval and rebels against disapproval and advice, because to him any criticism indicates his failure, and he wants to think well of himself. His demand for independence becomes rather fierce at times; when opposed or given orders, he may act in a daring and defiant manner to express his independence. He demands the right to choose his own friends and to devise his own amusements.

His deeply felt need for independence is a necessary part of growing up, of learning to make decisions, solve problems, and face certain perils and temptations. The desire for self-expression becomes so pressing at times that the forbidden becomes attractive merely because it is forbidden. Seeking the forbidden may bring the culprit no true pleasure, but its daring may bring a thrill. Such defiance is not delinquency. If repeated too often because of the thrill of its danger, however, it can lead to delinquency. Nor is it a sign of maladjustment. The maladjusted child deliberately commits deeds he knows will bring dire results. But the normal adolescent's deeds are merely a gesture of defiance. He may later regret them but wouldn't for the world admit it. That would lower his dignity. Instead, he may voluntarily cut the grass or take a bath without raising a row. Parents do well to accept this flag of truce, unless the deed well deserves punishment.

A girl may feel a sense of rebellion as deeply as does a boy, but she expresses it less openly. When deeply frustrated, she may weep bitterly and put on a scene; or, she may become stubborn and resentful and may sulk. Although she may be greatly peeved at having to stay home and study while the other girls go to a movie, she can see a good reason for the command. However, being forbidden to wear high heels, have a permanent, use lipstick, or stay out as late as her friends, makes her ashamed, not only of her own deprived self, but also of her depriving parents. When her father objected to her very high heels, Barbara, sixteen, exclaimed indignantly, "Do you whistle at girls in flat heels? Dad, don't be such a drip!"

Parents will find it difficult to deny a freedom to their daughter if this is a freedom which her companions enjoy. Every adolescent resents being different from others. I have observed that girls hemmed in by too many rules, or those who are given an unusual amount of work in the house, often leave home as soon as the law allows and try to get jobs out of town. Others may try to escape their bonds by marrying very young, even lying about their age to do so.

Under the stimulation of his hormonal activity, the emotions of the adolescent are intense and quite out of proportion to the incidents that arouse them. He vacillates between a silliness and an irritable grouchiness; now he is hyperactive and willing; next he is indolent and unresponsive. From high emotion he may quickly go "into the dumps." He soon realizes that his hysterical outbursts are socially disapproved, and he is ashamed of his lack of self-control when he wants to appear grown-up. If he responds to family and social controls and dams back the tide of his emotions, he may rid himself of the intense pressure within by strenuously exercising, which uses up his surplus energy; or, he may sulk for hours or even days.

For this reason, it is important that you encourage your youngster to participate in activities that provide an outlet for his energies. These can include sports of all kinds, dancing, or social events. You can get an idea of adolescents' excess energy by watching a group of them in a soda store or restaurant. They are loud and boisterous, whistling or singing, carrying on conversations by yelling across the room. They are having a wonderful energetic time.

Parents often wonder whether they are overly strict or overly indulgent toward their teen-agers. It would be well to remember that giving your child the freedom he needs also may entail giving him license to do things to which you object. Standards vary in different sections of the country, and even within different economic groups in the same towns.

In one high school, for instance, all dances end at ELEVEN P.M. Parents call for the children, and the youngsters come to the cars when the music stops. The parent who brings his child home at 11:30 is doing exactly the same as other parents; he is conforming to the standards of the youngsters' environment and therefore is neither lax nor strict. In another school, dances go on until midnight. Since many youngsters drive their own cars, it is customary to go to a hamburger place afterward and dance for another hour or so to music from a juke box. In this instance, the parent who insists that his child come home at eleven is not conforming to the standards of this group and is being overly strict. But he would not be too strict if he required his daughter to come home at midnight.

Thus we can establish the only standard applicable: you should try to adjust, to some extent at least, to the conditions that are generally accepted among the child's companions, social class, school, and church in which you have placed him. You introduced your child to that setting. You cannot expect him to become an island. If the environmental conditions into which you have placed him are unsuitable, you have it within your power to change that environment. On the other hand, don't be a slave to your environment. Have some standards of right and wrong that you will maintain despite what others do.

When parents tell me that they are completely at a loss when it comes to understanding how to deal with their adolescents, I remind them that often the feeling is mutual: their teen-agers are similarly confused about how to deal with them.

The adolescent has many confusing social pressures bearing down on him, and many things he does unthinkingly turn out to be wrong. Sometimes it seems as if he just can't please anybody. For example, John's mother ordered him to be home from a party by ten-thirty. But the hostess didn't serve refreshments until ten, and then John was asked to take a girl home. If he had left on time, the jeering of his friends would have been harder to endure than the rebukes of his frantic mother and the denial of his allowance for a week. So John did not get home until eleven. The mother refused to listen to his excuse or consider its justification.

An adolescent who is rebuked for wrongdoing may either blankly refuse to explain why he acted that way, or offer a glib excuse. His sudden angry flare-up and destructive act may have been due to a hurt of some particular "sore spot," or a touching off of some smoldering grievance. If you severely punish him for refusing to explain, he may decide that it doesn't pay to refuse. The next time this happens, he may contrive an excuse too feeble to be convincing, or concoct a lie that sounds plausible. Of course, you want to know the reason for his bad behavior, but you should not drive him to lying. Lying is a cancerous disease; its growth is rapid and widespread and often incurable.

Where a parent-child relationship is well established and home life is happy, where parents are understanding and tactful, the rebellion normal at this age will be neither too frequent nor too serious. It is much better for your child to express rebellion and rage immediately than to give in to it merely inwardly and have worse consequences later.

An important part of growing up into responsible and happy adulthood is acquiring a tolerance of frustration. As I discussed in an earlier chapter, being able to tolerate disappointments and denials prevents a kinking of the personality. How well an adolescent endures frustration depends upon how often he has been denied in childhood and whether he has been able to find satisfactions that compensate for his disappointments. If he can tolerate frustration, it means that he accepts the fact that disappointments are inevitable and can be faced bravely without the loss of his self-esteem. Unless the adolescent can feel responsible for failures resulting from his own choices and his own deliberate acts, he may conjure up false excuses (rationalize), instead of learning from these experiences. This tendency can lead to his refusing to accept the consequences of his own acts; someone else is always to blame.

Adolescence is a romantic age, when the young person does a great deal of daydreaming. This is entirely normal. Daydreaming is his way of escaping from reality and of attaining pleasures he knows are impossible, at least for the present. In his daydreams the boy may become a great general decorated for deeds of valor; or an engineer noted for his bridges and edifices; or an intrepid space pilot, the first to reach the moon. His daydreams may be of less glory—he tops his class in honors, he is mayor of the town, or he is a great lover among beautiful women. In these daydreams, the world revolves around him; nothing exists except that which affects him. Nothing is denied him; he gives all the commands.

A girl may daydream that she is a popular socialite, one of the ten best-dressed women, a queenly person respected for her beauty and poise. She marries a handsome man and has a fine home, where she is an envied hostess. She takes trips to faraway places, traveling deluxe as featured in the advertisements. If she is a poor student, she may dream of sailing victoriously through her examinations and astounding her teachers; if a serious student, she gains the highest honors.

A boy's daydreams may be sexual in content if he is overstimulated sexually or has been initiated into sexual relationships. He may dream of despoiling a girl who has rejected or ridiculed him. The boy should be taught that it is against God's law to give deliberate consent to such desires even though there is no bad action. The girl's daydreams have little to do with sex, though she may be in the arms of the most popular boy and exchange kisses with him, or she may be pursued by many and have to single out a favored one, or she may be a marvelous dancer and the boys all try to cut in at dances.

These daydreams bring the fulfillment of unsatisfied desires. In them, the unloved child is cherished; the unnoticed child is eagerly sought after; the neglected child turns out to be the most talented, etc., etc. The child who has been punished may dream of dying; everybody weeps beside the casket, sorry for having been unkind. Cora envied a girl who played the piano at parties. Cora herself had a "tin ear," but in her daydreams she sang so beautifully that crowds gathered outside her house to listen to her. An anemic boy continually pushed around by other boys daydreamed that as a coach he bawled out the big pitchers and catchers and as an iron-nerved sergeant he led his company through a hail of lead.

Thus, the adolescent's daydreaming brings consolation, moments of complete happiness and wish fulfillment. It makes life more tolerable for the rejected, unloved child by affording him love and appreciation and appeasement for his despair. So while daydreaming often exasperates a parent or teacher, it may be serving some good purpose in helping to relieve tensions which press in on the adolescent from every side.

Downed by his discouragements, the adolescent may escape more and more often into the dream world, however, and return to reality with more and more difficulty. Finally, he may fail to return and instead live entirely in a world of fantasy; in this case, he is a hopeless psychotic. More commonly, the adolescent who often retreats into a dream world merely becomes highly imaginative.

Such a person was Grace, a shy little girl who would walk home from school with a group of girls and eat lunch with them. Her friends liked her but always forgot to include her in their parties. Occasionally, Grace would invite them to a wonderful party to be given at a swanky club, with a fine orchestra, beautiful flowers, and splendid refreshments. She named the boys who had already said they would come, boys whom the girls looked at longingly but had not met. The date was always vague and always postponed because of her mother's illness or some other valid reason. The girls who had eagerly awaited this party began to realize that Grace's dream would never come true.

Some daydreamers become inveterate liars. To hear her tell it, Mary, a bright but very homely girl, visited the homes of the very wealthy, went yachting with them, and rode to the hounds. She had an expensive new hat when another girl had one, but her mother wouldn't let her wear it to school. When someone's relative went to California, Mary's sister had just gotten back from Europe. Her lies harmed no one and they carried no malice—they merely made the other girls jealous until they found her out. Mary's daydreams kept her from feeling deprived and frustrated; she bolstered her pride by bragging.

It often comes as an emotional shock when youngsters realize that they cannot go to college. Since colleges can admit only a small portion of their applicants today, they pick and choose. So while the youngster with exceptionally high marks is usually accepted, one with above average marks may be rejected because he lacks "personality plus." He may not have been elected to any high school offices because he was not sufficiently popular; or, he may not have excelled in any sport and thus is not an "all-around-person."

This attitude taken by many colleges can be very unfair to worthy youngsters. One may have devoted all his time to his studies, determined to get college grades. Another may have been too shy to be popular; or, it may have been necessary for him to work after school hours, thus eliminating time for social life. The rejected student should be told that the world need not end just because he cannot attend college. He can take special studies in extension, if there is a college nearby. He can study at home—it *is* possible, even if very hard. If he must work to help support the family, he should know that it is never too late to enter school. Parents and teachers who know that the adolescent wants to go to college, but lacks funds, should seek advice regarding possible scholarships. And while the youngster is in his early years in high school, they should urge him to work for marks that will make a scholarship possible.

CHAPTER SEVEN

Adolescent "Stress and Storm"

Why Teen-Agers Act That Way

The theory that adolescence is inevitably a time of deep and serious stress and storm is largely discounted today. Many adolescents go through this period without drastic upset or permanent trauma. To some, adolescence is very upsetting. The inner drive and exciting new experiences that come with the maturing process bring an enrichment of emotions, an awareness and evaluation of joy and sadness. The new vigor gives a desire to be continually "on the go," and the pepped-up youngster welcomes any excitement and bounces about until he drops from sheer fatigue. He finds it difficult to adjust to the requirements of society and does many thoughtless things.

For example, a boy and girl sat in a parked car, watching the moon and listening to the radio. With the girl's head on the boy's shoulder, they fell asleep. An understanding policeman shook them awake and told them to go home and never do that again. Had he made an issue of their parking at the late hour, the teen-agers might have suffered from parental wrath and the implied disgrace. While the girl involved knew that disregard for society's conventions could harm her reputation, she may not have known that her conduct presented possibilities of temptation.

Few teen-agers realize that the fun of doing silly or ridiculous things just for the sake of excitement can bring disaster. Two young couples were walking around town on a starry night, enjoying the crunch of the snow beneath their feet. Suddenly they began to snowball passing street cars. It was great fun until one snowball that was aimed too high crashed through a window and a passenger was severely cut by the broken glass.

"I didn't think" is often the excuse of the adolescent, as in the case of the teen-agers returning home from high school who stopped to play on the platform of a railroad station. One boy tossed another's books onto the tracks. The second boy climbed onto the tracks to retrieve the books and failed to see an express train approaching. He was killed instantly.

Young people should be taught that the rules of our society are based, not upon priggishness, but upon the need to strengthen our self-control and prevent enticement into tempting situations. For example, a girl who has been taught to respect her integrity will demand that respect from others. If she does not submit to being mauled, she will not be called upon to fight off temptation. Adolescents should be told that emotional control means *mastery* of impulses and passions; it does not mean suppression of emotions, happy or unhappy. Suppression of emotions leads to aggressive acts in some individuals; in others, it may produce a colorless personality, which is dubbed "jerky" or boring.

A typical teen-ager extends his sense of humor; he laughs easily and often at very simple things. He may do anything for a laugh, but if that laugh in any way derides him, his ego rebels. Very few are sports enough to enjoy a laugh on themselves.

To prove this point, I recall the case of an unusually tall boy who got into trouble with the police. This boy did the barest minimum of work to remain in his high school class. The teacher reproached him constantly but received only a sullen response. One day the teacher warned the boys against smoking. "I don't know if many will take my advice," she said. "Some of you are too dumb to know what is good for you. For example, Joseph here," pointing to the tall lad; "if he were as tall as he is dumb, he would be able to smoke cigarettes on the moon." The rest of the class laughed heartily, and Joseph sat in red-faced silence. After class, when he saw that no one was looking, Joseph collected a pile of rocks and broke eight windows of the school.

The parent of an adolescent girl should resign himself to the fact that she may giggle or weep at any time and often with very little reason. Two teen-age girls were sprawled on the floor, listening to the radio. One said, "I feel just like screaming." The other said, "Well, let's scream." They screamed and screamed. Then they got up and ran when the man of the house came thumping down the stairs. They hadn't a thing to scream about; they were just letting off steam. A girl may also complain of feeling blue, but she can't explain why. A trivial event—a word, in fact—may tilt her emotions either way.

Boys at this age have disdain for girls who giggle, but they themselves give out loud haw-haws, which can be equally annoying. In order to release pent-up emotion they may whistle or loudly sing snatches of songs with utter lack of harmony and disregard for others' ears, or yell at games. Girls scream at games to attract attention, to ape the boys, or merely to tune in to the excitement. If you complain of the racket caused by the young revelers, you may very well be talking to deaf ears. A girl may exclaim, "Oh, mother!" and wonder if her parent was ever young. To the young, being loud seems entirely normal.

Some emotions are constructed to serve special purposes. When intensified, however, they may bring unhappiness and in some cases lead to abnormal behavior. Fear is such an emotion. It is an inner traffic light, which gives a go-ahead signal and a stop warning. It has a primitive purpose in animals and man: it warns of threatening danger and elicits an instinctive life-preserving reaction.

An adolescent is less concerned with perils that may threaten his life than is the younger child, because the older one has learned that there are protective measures. The teen-ager's fears are emotional rather than instinctive. He no longer looks for a burglar under the bed or sees ghosts at the window. In fact, he may be thrilled by darkness. Except in early adolescence, the terror movies he sees on TV may bring shivers, but rarely personal fear. Put a youngster in a boat and he may rock it recklessly; he may dash through the country in "hotrods" at speeds that would curl the hair of an adult; he may daringly walk over railroad bridges; he may swim into the highest breaking waves. He enjoys these thrills most when he is with others; they would be unattractive if he were alone.

Despite his outward show of bravado, he does have fears which worry him, even terrify him, and which may leave scars on his personality. Mostly, these fears are anticipated but rarely realized: adolescents cross many bridges never reached. Unless he lives in a deprived home, his fears are not financial; he blithely assumes that somehow his parents will work out family budgets. He does not worry about whether money will be forthcoming for some much-desired pleasure; he may invite a girl to an expensive dance without a nickel in his pocket. Fear of getting sick or of dying rarely occurs to him, unless his life is imperiled.

What, then, are the fears of adolescents? Some are deeply ingrained fears—fear of injury by mechanical devices, or fear of attack by evil persons, for instance—which have been given them by their overly solicitous mothers. Some youngsters never cease to be afraid of swings, elevators, planes, or any device that lifts them from the ground. When they complain of seasickness, in most cases it is fear which has caused the gastric upset. Some adolescents, particularly girls who have been repeatedly warned about people attacking them, are fearful of all strangers.

Fear of physical punishment usually ends at adolescence; a youngster whipped at this age may resent it bitterly. Most often he fears punishment by deprivation because he anticipates pleasures so intensely. Loss of his weekly allowance is very serious to an adolescent, for he usually needs every dime to meet the social demands of his particular group. Fear of censure also can be great, either because he craves the parent's approval, or because explosive anger and nagging shatter his sensitive nerves. Often a teen-ager says he would rather take a licking than have his parent berate him verbally for a long period. However much a tongue lashing is feared, it rarely serves as a deterrent; the youngster subjected to such constant nagging grows up fearing a bawling out from those in authority. He cringes before his boss, never gaining entire confidence in his own ability or in the fairness of his supervisor or employer.

Fear of the law is a healthy one for adolescents to have. It normally brings respect for the law and prevents yielding to temptation. To the delinquent, however, fear of the law is unattended with respect; he fears only being caught. Yet even this fear may deter him from crime. The adolescent with high moral values will not commit a major crime. However, unless he has acquired an appreciation of laws forbidding minor crimes, he may blissfully disregard them. He may drive at reckless speed, delighting in his skill; if he should kill someone accidentally, he will no doubt be overwhelmed at the result of his carelessness and feel guilty because of the injury he has done. But that speeding itself is a crime is a point of view he may not accept.

Children who have fear of flunking an examination may be spurred to cram; thus their fear may help them pass. Fear usually haunts those who know they are ill-prepared, even though they forget their fear between examinations. Often fright will make a student's mind go blank; he cannot answer questions he knows. Other students bone up at the last minute, only to become confused. Some children become sick just before an examination; some become truants at this time; some quit school and refuse to go back.

The poor student is not the only one unnerved by the prospect of examinations: the ambitious student who fears a competitor or who desires a high mark to please the family or himself will suffer equal terror. Such children often develop tics and other compulsive mannerisms. John was typical of this type. He became so keyed up that every sudden sound startled him. He found it increasingly difficult to sleep. His classmates ridiculed him for griping whenever he failed to receive an "A plus" in a course, and he annoyed his teachers by his protests that they were unfair in giving him anything less than a perfect mark. John was destined to be a worrier all his life. Unless his personality changed radically, he would never succeed to his own satisfaction.

A child may hold up a serene mask which hides constant fears concerning family troubles. For example, he may deeply fear the increasing alcoholism of his father, the shame of a mother who is "talked about," the waywardness of a sister or a brother. Often the obvious poor health of this frightened child is difficult to explain on physical grounds; it may be dismissed as "growing pains." Children generally grow to fear those actions of their parents or other family members of which they are ashamed.

Fear of social inadequacy and disapproval also is frequent in adolescents. They long for popularity among their own group; some youngsters who have a simple home environment and are therefore unable to keep up with the Jones' children, believe themselves to be unpopular and unappreciated. They may be ashamed to bring friends into their home because they are ashamed of their parents, though they love them. They may fear that other children will find out how uneducated or uncouth their parents are. This unfortunate bitterness may permanently scar their personalities. One boy who had come from a poor home became a highly successful businessman. He bought a suburban house for his parents and gave them a generous allowance. But he made certain that his parents were never around whenever he entertained business associates.

Some adolescents, like many adults, exhibit a bravado to conceal a fear arising from lack of self-confidence. They fear the unexpected—anything they are unprepared to face—and they fear anything new that will disturb whatever security they have. Usually these are overprotected children, who have never faced problems alone and have never had responsibilities. They grow up pretending great self-satisfaction, but actually they need constant support.

The emotional stress produced by all these unrelieved fears and their accompanying anxiety may cause a mental sickness which has bodily symptoms—what we know as a psychosomatic disease. The bodily changes occur in response to the mental distress: the pulse quickens, tightened nerves cause trembling, sweating or shivering, loss of appetite, nausea and diarrhea. Continued headaches, or fatigue from sleeplessness give evidence of some disturbing bodily illness, but actually there is none. However, this is not malingering, nor is it a pretended illness to gain sympathy. The victim is really suffering. For this reason, an adolescent's fears should be more than lightly regarded. If reasoning with the youngster brings no adjustment, psychiatric help should be obtained.

A prolonged anxiety state which produces symptoms such as I described above can lead to serious maladjustment and psychoneurosis. The cause of the underlying fear must be determined and the anxiety relieved. Inasmuch as the personality disturbance exhibited by a maladjusted child is evidence of his struggle to establish himself as an individual against insurmountable odds, he requires special care and assurance of security and love. A youngster's anxiety may not arise from the denials or repression of his own personal desires; it may arise from tensions produced by an inadequate or unhappy home. Even when this condition exists, it must be handled with care. Occasionally, the court has to remove a child from surroundings which make him neurotic or delinquent; yet the shock to the child can be very great. A teenage boy who had developed pronounced neurotic behavior as a result of home conditions was asked by a judge to choose between his two parents, who had decided upon a divorce. Unable to decide, he was given to his mother. This boy's pride in himself and in his family was severely hurt. He felt insecure and fearful of his future—and his neuroses were worse than before.

The tragic result of adolescent fear sometimes is suicide. A few decades ago, more girls than boys committed suicide because of their fright and shame about pregnancy without marriage. Today girls have more information about such matters. They are aware of the danger and of the need for self-control and for fighting off temptation. Moreover, more institutions are equipped to house these unfortunate mothers during their confinement and to arrange for adoption of the babies.

Today more boys than girls commit suicide. These are maladjusted children, though usually not delinquents. It takes daring to be a delinquent; this may carry him through his trial and judgment. He wants to fight back, and ending his life does not appeal to him as a way out. It is the maladjusted child who inadvertently gets into trouble and is unable to face the accusations of society who may seek an escape by taking his life. The adolescent who is intensely unhappy because of lack of love or because he feels utterly insecure may also seek this escape.

Domineering parents who prevent their child from participating in adolescent joys, who criticize, nag, and constantly misinterpret his actions, can drive a sensitive child to suicide. The shamed and heartbroken parent will disclaim all guilt. "I tried to raise him as a good boy," they say—and they believe it. Recently the newspapers reported that a child committed suicide because he failed in a school examination. I doubt it. Experience teaches that few if any suicides are committed on the spur of the moment because of a single unhappiness. The desperate escape has long been considered; the newest frustration—the apparent cause—is merely the last straw.

Sixteen-year-old Marietta was the daughter of hardworking, prosperous immigrants who clung to Old World ways. She went to the movies only in the company of her parents or her brother, who usually didn't want her along. A plain girl with heavy features, Marietta was allowed no permanent and had to wear her hair slicked back in a bun. Her homemade clothes were unfashionable. Although she had some girl friends, they never invited her to their parties. And boys never looked her way.

Then Marietta fell in love with a charming college boy, who worked in a grocery Saturday nights. Marietta always asked him to wait on her. He was amused at her obvious "crush" and treated her kindly. At first she hoped he might ask her for a date, but dating this unattractive girl of a lower class never entered his mind. When Marietta realized that her love was hopeless, she became moody and strangely quiet. But no one paid attention to her frequently repeated soft words, "I think it is beautiful to die."

One Sunday afternoon, she passed this boy with a pretty girl on his arm. He glanced at Marietta and did not recognize her. The stricken girl went home and wordlessly plunged to the floor at her mother's feet. She never left her bed, seldom spoke, rarely opened her eyes, and refused to eat or drink. She was taken to a mental hospital and forcibly fed, but in a little while she died. The physical cause of her death was given as dehydration and starvation, but it was, in effect, suicide. Her sweet-faced mother said in broken English, "I don't know how Marietta could do this. She was such a good girl and we loved her so and gave her a good home."

Philip, aged fifteen, was another troubled child, who refused to go to school after he had been in one grade several years. He was bitter about the death of his mother, who had always babied him, and about his father's second marriage. To his stepmother he was surly and disobedient and resented every criticism. He learned to threaten to kill himself whenever he was rebuked; his frightened stepmother then gave in to him. A neighbor laughed at her one day and said, "He won't kill himself. He's just trying to scare you. Next time he says that, you just lay down some papers and tell him to go ahead but stand on the papers and not get blood on the rug." The next time Philip yelled at her, "I'll kill myself," she followed that suggestion. The boy went upstairs and shot himself with his father's gun. Unfortunately, the adolescent who talks of suicide may be serious about it.

It can be said as a general rule that the most severe cases of stress and storm occur mostly in oversensitive, maladjusted, or delinquent children. The tension is a result of the child's frustration from denied desires, or from the parents' misunderstanding of the motives behind the child's demands. A youngster accorded only limited freedom, who has not learned habits agreeable to social codes, and who is denied adult status, can become so frustrated when his emotions run high that he is propelled into aggressive acts which he well knows are unacceptable. Remember that he is motivated by a desire to stand out as a *person* and be recognized as such.

If you have tried to deal with your youngster in the light of modern-day knowledge and remain bewildered, fearing the worst yet to come, you probably should seek psychiatric help. To simply call the child uncontrollable is unfair. Unless a psychosis lies beneath the unacceptable behavior, the cause of his difficulty can be readily discerned, and with your help the mixed-up adolescent can be restored to normal, happy behavior.

Moral Values of the Adolescent

Religious ideals and motives are useful in cultivating strength of will and control of the emotions and temptation. The adolescent's religion should be a sustaining faith in order that his relationship to God does not suffer during these years of fluctuating emotional development and changing experiences.

Adolescence is the age of highest inspiration and aspiration. Parents who have given religious training to their preadolescents—at a time when children accept such teachings without question—need have little fear that the emotional upheavals of adolescence will seriously shake established religious beliefs. Many youngsters go through a period of questioning and doubt, or through a religious overemotionalism, which may seem irrational, but except for changes in certain details of belief, their religious faith will probably continue into adulthood.

Along with changes in social thinking, the adolescent may question what his elders teach about the wickedness of movies, dances, smoking, card playing and drinking. Adolescents tend to act and think like the majority of their teen-age associates. If too great pressure is brought upon them by their parents, the children may reject their elders.

This point is exemplified in the case of a teen-ager who did not know how to dance and, as a result, was missing out on the good times of her group. When she began to attend dancing school, a woman in her church warned her sharply that dancing was sinful. The girl replied earnestly, "I'm having a tough time learning to dance and I'm ashamed of my clumsiness. So when I'm dancing, I ask God to help me. Seems to me it doesn't matter where I go if I take God along."

The narrow-minded woman gave her up as lost, and had her removed as teacher in the church kindergarten because of her bad influence. Grievously hurt and disillusioned, the girl stopped attending that particular church. To the bigoted woman this seemed proof that dancing was leading to a downfall. Of course it never did, and although this experience shook the girl's faith in "professors of religion," her religious faith held firm.

The preadolescent is aware of the difference between right and wrong. His conscience leads him to weigh the consequences of his behavior; he knows that unhappiness, perhaps even a penalty, follows wrongdoing. The adolescent, however, likes to deliberate; when he chooses the right it is not only because parents and society demand it, but also because he may have reverence for the law of God. His fear of wrongdoing and its consequences is even stronger than before; but now he is less concerned with avoiding the wrong than he is with doing the right.

Choosing the right is not always easy for the adolescent. Consider, for instance, how the tenets of the home, the church, and of society are not in accord regarding cocktails. Adults disagree so greatly in their views of what is acceptable conduct that the adolescent is perplexed. He is told that he should not drink. What should he think if his own father comes home intoxicated? Making light of such an occurrence does not reassure him, does not reestablish his admiration for a beloved parent; especially, it does not assure him that religion deters wrongdoing. He may reason that if certain things are right for his parents, why are they not all right for him?

In this regard, the parents' example is all important. A child may stretch his conscience and do something he feels is wrong, such as telling a white lie to help out a friend, but he expects his parents to be infallible. A boy who accidentally tore a page in a library book asked his mother if he would have to pay for it. She patched the page with transparent tape and said nobody would notice. Such twisting of a code confuses the young mind and is hardly a guide for honest adulthood. The youngster's religious beliefs may be so well rooted that though he may lose faith in his parents' perfection, his faith in God pulls him through.

While most teen-agers remain grounded in the religion of their families, a few may question and flounder, show an intolerance of dogma, and perhaps lose their faith, which, in time, may return unaltered or be discarded. Since this is a time of intense emotional needs, children whose early religious training has been limited may seek the help of their parents' church, become converted, and accept religion as a way of life. The adolescent who has a firm belief in his Maker and tries to follow the teachings of his faith, bravely faces the stresses of his changing world.

In addition to his religious beliefs, the teen-ager's code includes many social taboos about which you probably have no idea, or may regard as nonsense. He sets up standards for himself which he expects you to follow. For example, he may have been taught as a preadolescent that it is despicable to read mail addressed to other people; therefore, he thinks it despicable if anyone reads his. Many parents offend in this way.

I am thinking of a couple who would deny that they refused the right of ownership to their child. Yet when their fifteen-year-old girl did not offer to share a letter, they assumed it contained something objectionable, hunted for it, and read it. This practice led to an unfortunate incident. Their daughter, Emily, had met a boy when she was visiting out of town. They found they enjoyed many of the same things. The girl enjoyed his letters and showed them to her chum, but she did not show them to her parents. They were perfectly innocent letters without a suggestion of love-making in them.

One day the girl was astonished when the boy wrote to her, enclosing a ridiculous letter from her father. The parent had misconstrued a recent letter the boy had written and told him not to write again or he would report him, not saying to whom.

Emily was bitterly ashamed of her parents. She was too embarrassed to write the boy again. When later she married and was divorced, she blamed her parents for their interference. The boy with whom she had broken off had become a fine man; she believed that if it had not been for her father, she might have married him.

Individual Differences

Each child has individual differences in his attitudes toward school and society. He has different motives, aspirations and goals. Therefore, no two children can be treated in exactly the same way, nor can they be expected to react alike to all influences exerted upon them. A child cannot be exactly fitted into a molded pattern.

Individual differences between children of the same age group become strikingly apparent during adolescence. Besides variations in physical development, there are broad differences in personality, character, and experience. The differences in temperament, in motivation, and in sensitivity you may have noted in preadolescence are intensified in adolescence. Influences producing these differences include, not only heredity, family background and environment, but also inner factors such as special abilities, talents, and interests; types of training and rearing; and all past experiences which have brought either gratification or disappointment.

A child's intelligence grows continuously up to the age of thirteen, sixteen, or even twenty, and the rate of growth is in proportion to his age. As his intelligence grows, he acquires the ability to grasp ideas and to think abstractly. For example, when we learn history, we learn of chronological events; this is factual learning. In order to understand why these events took place and why people act as they do, however, we must think abstractly. The ability to do this type of thinking increases with age, experience, and education, according to the intelligence with which the individual is equipped. For this reason, we can sometimes observe that the adolescent who begins his advanced studies later than normal often progresses much more quickly than those who start at the average age.

What native abilities you should expect from your child will depend to some extent upon his Intelligence Quotient (IQ). The results of an IQ test are not always accurate, since these tests are designed for children reared in fairly normal conditions. For instance, the child of immigrant parents, or one raised in an isolated community, lacks the education acquired by the typical American child and therefore, according to the IQ standards, will score lower than normal.

Delinquents are often considered to have less than normal intelligence; those who are subnormal are easy victims to bad influences. However, many individuals somewhat below normal intelligence become self-respecting, self-supporting citizens. On the other hand, many adolescents with normal or superior intelligence become delinquents through improper rearing. While they may excel in their studies, they are below average in moral values. Delinquents of high IQ can devise crimes that require superior cunning and skill and often use individuals of much less intelligence as their tools.

Parents are often heartbroken when they realize that their child is much below normal in intelligence. But these youngsters should not necessarily be considered helpless. Unless too subnormal, many individuals of low intelligence can hold jobs which are routine and support themselves and their families. Monotonous work does not annoy them as it does bright children, for they feel secure in their routine. Even those whose intelligence does not permit them to complete grammar school can be trained for useful work. They should not be humbled or ridiculed, for they need self-respect just as much as the brilliant ones. Often they are happy and good-natured, but if made to feel inferior they can be angered to the point of committing assault upon those who deride them.

If a youngster accepts his low intelligence, he can be reasonably happy. Ronald and Donald were twins who looked much alike. However, Ronald was slow. It was difficult for him to study, and often he fell asleep over his books. He was a placid boy who was not bothered by the fact that he was not highly intelligent. He dropped out of school and went to work in a factory. As he grew more skilled and his pay increased, he began to build a substantial bank account. Donald actually was not much brighter. But to prove to his parents and to others that he was not dull like his brother, he studied hard to keep up with his class. It was a struggle for him to graduate from high school. But now he could not bring himself to accept a factory job; he became a clerk at a much lower wage than his brother made. Because he cannot accept himself for what he is, Donald is chronically unhappy. But Ronald lives in serenity.

However low the intelligence of children, they always crave love. Low-grade morons who are trained to help in the home are happy in doing chores if in return they are praised and given treats such as candy and extra helpings. They are happier when busy and are less apt to get into trouble. They will get along all right as long as they are given no responsibility beyond their capabilities; but any change in their environment or routine upsets them. The moron is usually affectionate and accepts demonstrations of affection from anyone. For this reason, the subnormal girl is easily led astray. She is not immoral, but amoral; she has no understanding of the results of the sex act. Many prostitutes are said to be below normal in intelligence.

Subnormal adolescents should be watched carefully. I recall the case of two illegitimate children, a boy of fifteen and his sister, aged thirteen. Their mother worked at night as a cleaning woman and received some help from the city. She came home early each morning, set out breakfast for the children, whom she had put to bed before she left for work, then went to bed herself. Their intelligence was too low for them to attend school, so they played in the yard or in the house. Everyone was horrified when they learned that the children were about to become parents. The children were institutionalized. Of course, responsible people of the town should have concerned themselves before. They should have realized that the act of procreation demands no intelligence.

Children slightly below normal in intelligence should not be humiliated by being required to try to keep up in school with others of their age. They belong in special classes where they will progress more slowly. Teachers trained for this type of work have great patience; they try to help the child make his necessary emotional and social adjustments and develop his abilities so that he can attain that degree of success of which he is capable.

Some children do poorly in some subjects, but show special aptitude in other fields of study. Sometimes these young-sters are outstanding in the fields which interest them. They should have careful instruction in their poor subjects. They may be devoting too much of themselves to subjects which intrigue them and neglecting those of little interest.

Robert was such a boy. He could talk with surprising in-telligence on his collections of bugs, butterflies, and rocks, and he constantly visited the library seeking further informa-tion. He had an above-normal IQ, yet he failed in mathemat-ics, English and composition. His enraged parents considered throwing out the youngster's collections and demanding that his time and attention be devoted to his poorest subjects. But they wisely decided that in doing this, they might clip the wings of a possible scientist. Instead, they ruled that his in-terest be respected and encouraged, but that he be made to see that a one-sided education would not get him very far. Robert is now a more balanced student.

Parents who soon discover that their child has special tal-ents often insist that most of his time be given to lessons in his specialty. This is particularly true in the case of a child who is gifted musically. Although training in music should start early, other subjects should not be neglected if the child is to avoid developing a lopsided education and personality. Since many factors may prevent a person from earning a liv-ing in music—for instance, the pianist who loses the use of a hand must seek other work for a livelihood—the youngster faces a bleak future if his education has been limited only to music.

Does the IQ of an adolescent predict his eventual success as an adult? Many parents—those, naturally, of children with high IQ's—think so. However, success depends, not only upon intelligence, but also upon the ability to adjust to opportuni-ties and social demands, and to acquire and use the edu-cation and skill necessary for advancement. I know of several adolescents of above-average intelligence who were afforded all kinds of opportunities to excel. Instead, they became mediocre adults, isolated in their self-centered, narrow little world, where they held themselves superior to everyone else. They were unapproachable, unloving and unlovable. One in particular had an extraordinary intellect, a superior education, but an inferior personality, which unsuited him for taking a role of importance in the community. A neighbor with a normal IQ, but with a well-integrated personality, far surpassed the brilliant, unadjusted one. In this respect, adolescent experiences are those of adult life; for the adolescent with a talent for leadership does not necessarily have the highest scholastic ability. Personality is a considerable factor in his success.

Teen-Age Delinquency

The delinquent, like the poor, we always have with us. Cain killed Abel because he was jealous of his younger brother, and became a fugitive and vagabond. Thus the first child in the Bible was also a delinquent. But that the delinquent who has "wasted his substance with riotous living" can come to his senses and be reclaimed is also told in the Bible, in the story of the prodigal son.

Juvenile delinquency seems to be increasingly prevalent. This is partly due to our great increases in population and our huddling in large cities. Newspapers feature stories of misdemeanors and crimes committed by the young offender, apparently because people like to read them and shake their heads over them. It seems that today's adolescent knows how to get away with more than the youngster of a decade ago. We should recognize that the delinquent is one who not only breaks a law, but is apprehended. There are many delinquents who are equally guilty but who are not found out; they do not suffer the humiliations imposed by the law.

To understand this problem properly, you should realize that the teen-ager is aggressive and adventurous by nature. He still fears his father's strap, but running from a policeman is fun; being arrested and dismissed with a warning brings admiring attention from his less daring pals; it also serves as a public notice he has craved ever since he claimed his independence as an individual. He gets his name in the paper, and this, in his view, may be an accomplishment.

Delinquency can be recognized and treated early, at which

time it is curable. But if it is allowed to grow, it can bring lifelong misery. Most boys who become delinquents first go through the "swiping" age, not because they specially desire what they steal, but because the daring brings a thrill. There are several reasons why a youngster may steal—because his parents have denied him something he desired, for "no good reason," or "just to be mean." He may go no further than this stage because corporal punishment or threats of reprisal by law deter him, or careful religious training has made him realize that stealing is repugnant.

Probably 90 per cent of delinquency in this age group involves stealing cars. When I was a boy, we had bicycles. Many were stolen—the majority, of course, were not—but the value of the stolen bicycle usually was not great enough to make a court case of it. However, now when a boy steals an automobile, the value of today's cars makes the theft grand larceny.

Some boys do not steal cars to make money. Rather, they simply want to use them for a while and either return them to the owner or leave them where they will be recovered. However, even if his motives are relatively innocent, the lad apprehended with a car which does not belong to him faces criminal prosecution. Even at this stage, a youngster treated with understanding may realize his error and grow into responsible adulthood.

However, if his offense is serious, often the adolescent is sent to a reform school. Whether or not there is lasting reform depends upon the type of school, how deeply ingrained the delinquency has become, and the public's reaction to the offender when he is discharged, perhaps on parole.

The juvenile delinquent suffers from a deep-seated personality disturbance. For one or several reasons, he has failed to adopt the social standards and code of his community and has rebelled against them. His asocial behavior results from a long-continued nervous strain and tension and a frustration beyond his tolerance. He has no goal in life, no ambition for success as a respected individual, no hope of acceptance as a person. To himself he is all important; but he believes he is not important to anyone else. Therefore, his behavior is an attempt to escape from the pressures of a world which not only hurts him but also curbs every desire and prevents him from becoming an independent individual.

The child who is reared in a home where poverty is ever pressing, where every comfort and even many needs are denied, may have as his only playground the streets and alleys of an unsavory neighborhood. There he comes into frequent contact with criminals, prostitutes, gamblers, dope peddlers, sex offenders and alcoholics. His playmates come from equally distressing homes. Even though the danger that he and his companions will become delinquents is great, most of these children do not become delinquents. Thus we can conclude that while the adolescent raised under unfavorable conditions faces a hard struggle, the environment outside the home is not the chief cause of delinquency; rather, the home environment itself is the major factor which determines the way the child will go.

Delinquent parents—those who lead immoral lives, drink to excess, or are addicted to drugs—can hardly impart a moral sense to their child. Often such adults are so obsessed with their own needs that, never having wanted the child in the first place, they may reject him entirely. Since every child most of all needs love and a feeling of security, an adolescent denied these by his parents tries to get love from other sources. His older sister, grandparent, or other relative, an older person to whom he attaches himself—it may be a humble worker, a teacher, or a member of the Big Brother organization—may provide the affection he craves, wherein he can find security, a support in time of trouble. Thanks to such love, he may be saved from delinquency.

Since lack of security is the common characteristic of delinquents, it follows that they can come from all types of homes. Some are reared in homes which provide every luxury: others come from homes of extreme poverty, where even necessities are lacking. This cannot be overemphasized: it is more the kind of parents than the type of home that contributes to a child's personality.

In one home which provided more than usual comforts, where the parents were respected by their neighbors for their integrity, industry and dignity, the daughter grew up with high moral values, but the son became maladjusted and even a delinquent. Why did the son go wrong? Let us look at that family more closely. They were highly respected churchgoers. The father, who had "come up the hard way," was born in a large family, of hard-working parents, and left home early to earn his living. He worked endless hours, even long after he won financial success and respect as a heavy taxpayer. He expected the same effort by his boy, Peter; when he discovered that the lad was continuously in trouble in school, though he managed to get passing grades, he put Peter to work at his trade—work which the boy detested because he was unsuited to it. The father exacted absolute obedience and mercilessly whipped young Peter for the slightest disobedience. Although loyal to her husband, the mother wept over the welts on her son's back and rocked him, big boy though he was, in her arms.

Peter hated his father with an increasing fierceness. As soon as he came of age, he began to drink heavily. His mother agonized over him in prayer while he was out at night with the hoodlums of the town. Soon he was lost in the grip of drink. While his sister grew up to be a lovely person like her mother, Peter became a tramp and died in a brawl. For despite all that this home offered, the father's tyranny turned it into a hell for the boy.

Love is often denied the child of a broken home; hence, delinquency. Yet the child of a deserted parent may share a love with her that strengthens them both. A youngster reared by one parent and denied the love of the other parent may find a loving substitute for the lost parent. Or perhaps the one loving parent may give a devotion that is satisfying and protective. The child of a broken home faces many difficulties in his attempts to make a successful adjustment to society. His own married life may be rocky because of his deprived childhood.

I must also voice a warning to employed mothers whose children are left to roam the streets until the parent gets home, or are in the charge of an older daughter. The daughter may grow disturbed by her hard lot and seek to escape either by marrying or by running away from home. Her chances of becoming delinquent are great. The younger children likewise suffer from the lack of loving attention.

Some working mothers may leave their children in the care of an affectionate grandmother or other relative who gives proper care during the day. If these children are well guided and enjoy the mother's love when she is home, they may evolve as well-adjusted, happy individuals. In fact, they may even be better fitted to assume responsibilities than more sheltered children because they have been given a greater measure of freedom.

So, regardless of the kind of neighborhood the child comes from, or the degree of prosperity in his home, love and security provide an excellent shield against delinquency. The adolescent, in his determined efforts to establish himself as a person to be respected, wavers between his demand for emancipation from parental control and his need to retain his parents' love and security. He longs to be wanted and valued.

If you refuse to give up your control and continue to treat your adolescent as a child, he will not develop any responsibility. Moreover, if you deny him understanding and affection, he will feel rejected and inadequate. Frustrated, he may seek other satisfactions. He may become sulky, disobedient, and rebellious, and may in defiance commit asocial, aggressive, even unlawful acts. In this way he strikes back.

The unloved adolescent may hide his feeling of inadequacy, hurt, or unhappiness behind a bold bravado. He may pretend that he is tough in order to win the plaudits of his fearless, lawless gang. He may refuse to follow the dictates of society and even the dictates of his own conscience, rejecting society because it first rejects him. Of course, delinquency is ultimately the result of free choice and not of environment.

Almost always, adolescents whose delinquency brings them before the law have a poor relationship with their parents. If the parents have exerted too much authority, the adolescent usually fails to mature. He never acquires the ability to make decisions and meet responsibilities. Disappointments frustrate him easily because he is immature and does not profit from his experiences. The best protection against juvenile delinquency is to provide the young with good religious training.

Types of Adolescent Offenses

We have noted that stealing is the most prevalent misdemeanor in the early stages of delinquency. It usually begins with the snitching of things left lying around: for example, boys love to build carts and other objects and to erect clubhouses in the woods. They swarm around buildings which are in construction and help themselves to every accessible tool. They may literally wreck a vacant building, invariably smashing all windows, and carry away anything they can handle. What they can use or sell they hide away. Some parents applaud this type of thievery and may encourage their youngsters to bring home wood, coal or even groceries. Impoverished families may resent the good fortune of those better off than themselves and carelessly say, "The Lord helps those that help themselves." They can wink at petty thievery so long as the thief isn't caught, and their youngsters grow up believing that being caught is a greater disgrace than committing the crime. Occasionally a misguided parent or other adult will train a youth to shoplift, for which he will receive some small reward.

Purse snatching frequently occurs in big cities. It brings easy money and emulates the daring holdups committed by adults. Purse snatchers who read of holdups or see them acted out in movies seek that thrill for themselves.

An unhappy, frustrated child may also seek excitement by setting fire to a building: he experiences a secret thrill in watching the engines come, the firemen climbing ladders, the people crying over their losses.

Truancy is also a common misdemeanor among maladjusted high school students. It is safe to assume that frequent or habitual truancy has a definite cause, for a secure child has no desire to be a truant (his respectful attitude toward his parents extends to his teacher). But one who is unhappy at home may find no recompense at school for his disappointments and deprivation of affection: the behavioral pattern developed at home continues at school. The child expects the same rebuffs and indeed encourages them by his stubborn refusal to cooperate. If punished, he feels no incentive to do better; rather he is drawn to further opposition. He enjoys the turmoil he creates. In dealing with him, you may decide that he is as bold as brass; but actually he is a badly frightened animal at bay, striking out at all he believes to be his enemies. The habitual truant is seeking to escape his uncomfortable home and school environment. He may voluntarily return the first few times simply because he doesn't know what to do next; or, he may never return. Possibly he may establish himself in another city and obtain a job; or, perhaps he may become a bum.

Habitual truancy is preventable. When a child plays "hookey," his reasons should be uncovered. If he hates school, it may be because he can't keep up with his class and needs tutoring or special placement. If the teacher is "mean" to him, possibly she is too overworked or prejudiced to put up with a particularly bothersome child. Another possibility is that he is transferring to her the anger he feels against his parents. It should not be assumed that he can't learn; unless he is of low intelligence, he *can* learn. School should be made attractive to him; he should be influenced to "want" an education. Praise and rewards for any progress he makes will encourage him. If home conditions have led to the truancy, the parents, more than the boy, need guidance.

Truancy of a girl is very serious. If news of her truancy spreads, she might be suspected of laxity in sexual restraint, regardless of the truth. The truant girl who appears in public places when she should be at class is in grave danger, for she becomes an easy prey for depraved persons. Her truancy may ultimately lead to prostitution.

One of the most frightening types of adolescent offenses is drug addiction. Many of the addicts apprehended are minors, usually boys. They are deliberately recruited by the dope sellers. Usually they are first enticed with an offer of a marijuana reefer by another adolescent, who tells of the wonderful feeling they will get and dares them to try it. The smokers find it fun. Marijuana is not habit forming and can be given up without great distress. But now that he has started, the youngster is urged to try something that will give him a real kick. If he starts on this, he is in for deep trouble. He will need more and more to satisfy his craving. If he cannot raise the necessary money in a legitimate way, he may pawn some possession of his own or one belonging to his family; if more desperate, he may steal.

A youngster with little or no money to buy the drug may earn enough for his own needs by peddling it to others. If caught, these addicts usually refuse to reveal the source of their supply, fearing to be cut off from the drug. When they cannot get their shots, they suffer physical and mental torture. They lose weight, vomit, cannot sleep, and literally shake.

Drug addiction can lead to every kind of delinquency, not only because of the youngster's loss of moral sense and responsibility, but also because he will stop at nothing to get a new supply. The notion that addiction causes sex excitation and therefore leads to immoral sex relations is false. Girls who are denied the drug may sell their bodies to get a supply; having given in once or twice in desperation, they may consider themselves lost and no longer struggle against the new vice. In the same way, a boy may be led to homosexual practices. But the basic force at work is the desire for drugs, not a stimulation of the sex glands.

Parents, in these instances, rarely guess the reason for the change in their child. If anyone should suggest drug addiction, they would no doubt declare, "It couldn't happen to a child of mine." A parent may use home remedies when the youngster becomes listless, fatigued and dreamy, wildly excited, restless, or quarrelsome. Because the lad seems normal after his new dose of drugs, the parent, unsuspecting, may think the spell was just an adolescent upset. But this spell occurs again and again. Symptoms that occur when the drug is withheld (withdrawal symptoms) are so severe that the parent will become frightened and take the child to a doctor, who will recognize the trouble unless the youngster has secured a new supply and is calm again. Drug addiction can be cured, but the suffering during the withdrawal of the drug can be a truly terrifying experience. This type of delinquency is a sociological problem. The law should be aided in every way in running down those adults who use small children as decoys while they themselves hide safely away.

As shocking as drug addiction among adolescents are sex crimes and deliberate murders due to disordered sex feelings. They occur most often among teen-agers from bad environments, but are also committed occasionally by children of respected families. Sex crimes are never a first step in delinquency. They are a story in themselves and therefore will be discussed later, under the topic of sex disorders.

If you worry about the direction in which your child is heading, remember that delinquency can be prevented. A healthy parent-child relationship provides the needed love and security and respect for moral and social laws that will safeguard a youngster. If your child has engaged in the acts of an early delinquent, deal with him lovingly, kindly, and firmly, trying to correct whatever has led to his waywardness. If corrupting influences cannot be altered, he should be removed from them. Again, like some diseases, if delinquency is allowed to become deep-seated and chronic, it may become incurable. Even a psychiatrist may be unable to help when this stage is reached.

Sex Awareness: Its Problems

Many children arrive at the age of puberty unaware of its true purpose and meaning. This period, which cannot be denied or evaded, is common to all humans. It is a time when the body matures in readiness for the function of procreation.

The *problem* of sex in adolescence is a product of modern society. Primitive peoples have no such problem. When their children reach puberty, they are ready for sex activities. There is no prolonged waiting period. But in our culture, training of the child continues through the school years and well past the age of puberty. Thus, sex activity waits while we prepare the young person for the responsibilities of adulthood, guiding him into proper channels of thinking and acting, so that his adult behavior will be acceptable to society and in accordance with its laws and taboos and also in accordance with God's law.

Long before the formative and formidable years of adolescence, the child who has been properly instructed has learned the names and functions of his organs. He knows how babies are created and how they are born. This information was given gradually and naturally as his interest and curiosity regarding his own body developed. He also has been given a matter-of-fact awareness of maleness and femininity.

Now, at puberty, a new interest is aroused, one which is directed less to the anatomy of the organs and more to their specialized functions. Usually, children ask fewer questions of their parents at this time; but they get their information from other sources. They may whisper with members of their own sex, for example, and the child who received no information at home gets information from his age mates—much of it garbled, but all hush-hush and interesting. A boy listening to other boys boasting of their sexual exploits may manufacture some experiences of his own, in an attempt to outbrag the others.

Young boys learn masturbation practices early. Voluntary masturbation is a mortal sin for everyone possessing a normal, healthy mind and a free will, and parents should thus instruct their children. However, masturbatory practices during the period of puberty and adolescence should not be considered abnormal; this does little psychological harm unless someone fills them with fear of the consequences to their own bodies, such as impotency, infertility, or even insanity. Some boys find it not exciting but repulsive. It is no reflection on a boy's manliness if he does not relieve his sexual urges in this way.

Girls also whisper to each other, and listen in to adult conversations, particularly if the voices are lowered. They know more about sex, as a rule, because they read more, and while the early adolescent boy is reading adventure stories, the girl devours love stories. Girls mature at least two years earlier than boys, and while boys are still regarding members of the other sex as nuisances, girls are casting glances at them. But regarding sex, girls are usually "more proper" than boys. There are several reasons for this. Some mothers give their daughters the idea that sexual relations are a repulsive function to which wives must submit. For example, Lucy's mother explained nothing to her about the function of sex, but warned her that all males were wolves ready to pounce upon silly girls. Lucy was told over and over that she must never let men touch her; she must keep herself pure for marriage. Even Lucy's affectionate gestures toward her father were discouraged; they were considered a demonstration of sex. Her mother stood constant watch over her, fearing that she would "go wrong."

Lucy liked boys. She liked being kissed, but she did not understand the thrill she got when a boy's body touched her. She was without understanding when her sex feelings were aroused and was unprepared to control them. When she became pregnant, her furious, shamed mother turned her out of the house. The mother of the boy involved took her in, and a marriage was performed.

As this incident proves, keeping a girl ignorant of the nature of sex drives does not necessarily keep her pure and innocent. Both girls and boys should be taught the meaning and purpose of sex. They should be told that legitimate sex relations are a God-given means by which the two sexes propagate the race. This creative power should be jealously guarded against violation, and gratification of the urge should come only with marriage. The morals of self-control should be taught as naturally as the ideals of honesty and other morals —not as something fearful and secret.

Medical history abounds with cases reflecting the frustration and unhappiness that adolescents feel because of inadequate sex instruction. For example, there is the case of Joan N. When the first signs of menstruation appeared, she was terrified, believing she had injured herself. Her mother had failed to warn her of this coming event and instruct her as to its meaning and purpose. Like many foolish mothers, she then described it as a horrible curse that Joan must suffer in secret, like all women, every month.

This description only served to increase the girl's fears. She grew up shamed by her womanhood and entered marriage in terror. When she became pregnant, she was deeply shamed;

now everyone could see the result of evil passions. So she hid her pregnancy from the public eye and berated herself for having had relations with her husband. Her ignorance of sex was an undeniable factor in the ultimate break-up of her marriage.

Another example of how the lack of proper sex instruction can cause great harm is shown in the case of a mother who complained that her twenty-year-old daughter was apparently unable to secure dates with boy friends. The daughter shied away from all male companionship, although she had a strong desire to marry and raise a family. During the psychiatric interview, the daughter became emotionally disturbed and shouted to her mother, "When I was fourteen years old, you warned me to keep away from men because they would only get me into trouble. You told me over and over again that they would give me a bad disease and would make me pregnant for their own selfish motives. I believed you completely. Now after all these years, how can I change?"

Sometimes I wonder at the blindness of parents concerning their teen-ager's knowledge of sex. Once a mother brought an eighteen-year-old girl to my office because of some psychiatric disturbance. When the girl was outside, the mother asked me to avoid saying anything about sex, since her daughter did not know where children came from.

In another case, two very upset parents came to my office to tell me that their nineteen-year-old married daughter was pregnant. They were disturbed, they said, because she was a child, didn't know what pregnancy meant, and certainly knew nothing about raising children. I asked them if the marriage had been performed with their consent, and they said yes. Then I asked if they had expected their daughter and son-in-law to live like brother and sister. They were unable to answer.

At the child's adolescent stage, parents should seek the opportunity to chat alone with him occasionally: an evening stroll or drive with your youngster can be used as an occasion to discuss the psychology and temptations of sex.

Sooner or later you will encounter this question: should you tell your older adolescent boy or girl the details of marital intercourse, and if so, how and when should you disclose this information? Most sixteen or seventeen-year-old boys and girls will have learned these details by reading, hearing allusions in film and television shows, in chance conversations, and in other ways. However, unless your youngster broaches the subject himself, you may not know whether he has the proper knowledge. This subject is the most important of sex education and is probably also the most delicate.

As a general principle, I would advocate that complete instructions and details of marital intercourse are given before your children are twenty-one. The instruction should be given either by yourself, by a doctor or nurse of good ethical character, or by your pastor, if he feels qualified to do it and circumstances warrant his doing so. Perhaps the instruction may be given even better through printed matter that is completely in accord with good ethics.

At the present time, there is a widespread movement which advocates giving sex education to children in public groups, particularly in school classes. A serious objection arises in connection with such classes when the instruction is concerned, not with the virtue of chastity, but with the prevention of venereal diseases. Children are taught that sex abuses are evil, not because they are sins against the Creator, but because they tend to create disorder in the community. Despite this possible objection, however, teachers and school authorities often give excellent instruction from the physical standpoint.

I believe that such group instruction can serve a useful purpose if it meets three requirements:

1. A religious atmosphere should be present. Is mere knowledge of sex itself sufficient for the child? Certainly not. "The real reason for the general breakdown of personal morality is not that the boys and girls do not know enough about sex matters. They know too little about God," says one authority who has had much experience with the young. Knowledge itself is no virtue, although it is a necessary prerequisite to virtue. With the help of supernatural means children can obtain the self-control necessary for the practice of chastity. Education divorced from religious motives and principles

and imparted in a completely secular atmosphere is not sufficient for teaching the true nature of sex. Since such a milieu does not recognize sex as being a function related to God, it cannot treat sex crimes as being sinful; nevertheless, all sex offenses, whatever else they may be, are objectively sins against God. For this reason, sex education is best imparted in an atmosphere where recognition is given to the need of abiding by the moral law.

2. The teacher himself should be a mature individual, free from morbid, puritanical notions on the subject. The teenage lad should certainly learn to control himself and fight temptations, but he should also be told *how to learn* self-control. Emotional violence and tenseness in warding off temptations may not only have an effect opposite to that which is desired, but may also cause psychic trouble. Not our emotions, but reason and resoluteness must counteract and lead the sexual impulses. An impetuous youth finds it hard to learn the quiet approach to sexual temptations; that is precisely why he needs an experienced counselor. He should also pray for God's help.

3. The means devised and employed in imparting such instruction should be designed to give healthy and, at the same time, reverent attitudes. If the youngster is curious, he has a right to know the right answer. This answer should be complete enough to satisfy his present curiosity and be given reverently and matter-of-factly, without tension or anxiety on the part of the teacher. The sexes should be separated for these instructions.

Proper sex instruction should also avoid another danger—that of unilaterally overestimating the moral obligations concerning sex. By that I mean that the youngsters should not be given the impression that the Commandments relating to sex are the only ones that count.

In mid-teens the boy is no longer content with the companionship of boys only. His homogeneous outlook becomes heterogeneous, that is, bisexual. The first one of the opposite sex he loves is his mother, and at this age he demonstrates a new affection which delights her. If she does not recognize its meaning, or if she craves a love her husband denies her, she may respond with such strong affection that he may never be able to free himself from her possessive love. He may remain Mother's Boy and never quite grow up.

In the same way, the adolescent girl may surprise her father with embraces and lavish kisses. He should not be regretful when this ardor soon wears off, nor try to win it back. But if her overlove continues, her parents should recognize it as a manifestation of her awakening sex interest and gently lead her to friendly relations with the boys in her crowd. A girl's love for her father may become so intense that she takes up with older men. Usually these men are only amused and stand her off. But now and then one is flattered by the admiration of a pretty young girl, and a spring-fall love affair results, which the parents are unable to break up. Such marriages occasionally prove successful and are most likely to succeed if there are children.

As the adolescent boy begins to be attracted to the other sex, he becomes interested in grooming—in baths, in his hair, his shoes, and in his nails, if he happens to think of them. He begs his mother to press his pants and complains of the way she irons his shirts. This is the time of scented soaps and colognes and of outrageous clothes. His elders should not laugh at his efforts to enhance his appearance, or jibe at him for trying to shave, forgetting their own budding into adulthood.

Perhaps he was formerly scornful of dancing. But now he persuades a girl to teach him the latest steps. He dances fast and furiously. No dreamy stuff for him! If he is old enough to get a driver's license to operate a car, he begs for it constantly. If he has a license to drive only to school, he may cheat and drive at night if he looks old enough to fool the police. His driving is fast and reckless, but his keen coordination helps to avert many a near disaster. If he can't have the car, he and his girl may ride with another couple. But rarely would they ride to a dance or party with one of the old folks.

When typical teen-agers go to the movies, they usually sit at the rear, hold hands, or frankly neck. Since allowances are small, after the theater they modestly treat themselves to a soda or a hamburger and coke. Others of the crowd are there:

they pour dimes into the jukebox, and if space and the proprietor allow it they dance. They try to get home at the hour the parents set; otherwise, the girl may be penalized by not being allowed out for some time, and the boy's allowance may be stopped.

At this stage, youngsters mostly still travel in groups. They huddle together and sing, go on hikes and picnics, and attend dances. Going steady comes a little later.

This is a joyous time of life, one which is indeed memorable. If their child has been well trained in moral values, parents have no reason to sit at home desperately watching the clock and worrying. But of course the mother should know where her daughter is, with whom, and if she can be trusted to take care of herself.

Parents of youngsters in this stage of life should realize that the beauty of young romance is the subject of poetry and story. Its manifestations should not be smeared with suspicions of uninhibited sex. Sitting on the beach, in a parked car, or on a love seat at home, a girl and boy with their arms around each other may listen to the soft music of a radio, talk nonsense, laugh, and eat candy. This mutual attraction may suddenly quicken into love; most often it does not. It is rarely the dreamed-of one true love. Soon the theme song may be "Thanks for the Memory," and there is a change to other boys and girls. This is entirely normal, a step toward maturity.

The girl who is unduly affectionate, or who allows liberties such as having parts of her body touched, is often misjudged by the boy. Maybe she attaches no importance to such liberties, or permits them because other girls have told her that boys dislike prudes. But the boy's reaction is not what she expects. He may be disappointed in her, or even insult her.

Janet learned this lesson in a bitter fashion. She was raised in a very affectionate family. Her parents deeply loved each other and their children; they continually kissed, regardless of who was watching. The children, unless they were quarreling, also kissed frequently. They were looked upon as a very loving family. When Janet was a freshman at college, she met an attractive young man. They danced at a party and Janet was greatly fascinated by him. Later he took her home in his car, and in front of the dormitory door she affectionately kissed him good night. She waited for him to call again. He never did, for he concluded that her demonstration was an evidence of sexual desire and that she was "hot stuff." Actually, she was a splendid young woman.

If parents condemn necking and kissing, their children will probably dismiss them as old fogies who have forgotten their youth. But parents should firmly warn against any form of petting, which may lead to sexual arousal and capitulation. If the girl has learned respect for her person, she will find "pawing" repulsive. Boys should be trained to respect girls just as they want their own mothers and sisters respected.

A youth once remarked to me, "I'll neck all they want, but the girl I marry will be one who holds me off and slaps me if I get fresh." Girls should know that this attitude is ingrained in many boys. It is important to impress upon your daughter that a girl who is gracious and charming will have many dates but will not be on boys' lists as a "good necker." Doris was such a girl. One day a group of boys, who were standing in the hall, remarked on each girl as she passed on her way to class. Doris greeted them with a smile and a wave of her hand. One of the boys afterward repeated a compliment which she always treasured. One of the group had said of her, "There goes a girl—have all the fun you want, but don't get fresh." Fathers, even more than mothers, can give their daughters this understanding of boys.

"Crushes" are a natural phenomenon of adolescence. Youngsters may have a crush on someone of the same sex or age, or on an older, much admired person. A girl may have a crush on a handsome man, a popular figure, a movie star, or a man resembling her father. If not encouraged, crushes are soon over. But an older man who allows a young girl's crush to progress to the point of infatuation can do immense harm. Clarice, a motherless 16-year-old who adored her father, got a tremendous crush on an older man who came to the house occasionally. He was amused and flattered. She began to phone him and chatter; he responded by kidding her as a boy her own age might. One day she saw him park his car in front of a building; when he returned, she was in the seat. He took her to dinner, then drove into the country and parked. Her ardor convinced him that she was not the good little girl he had thought. She did not resist his sexual advances. When he learned she was pure and merely infatuated, he reproached himself for taking advantage of his friend's daughter. The girl's fright and remorse made her hate him and herself, and her disillusionment was complete. It was a shock from which she did not soon recover.

A boy in his late teens may have a terrific crush on a mature woman and sweep her off her feet with his love-making. If the flattered woman consents to marry him, his sex urge may be soon sated, and he leaves her. I vividly recall one such case. A handsome young man had been raised by his father and an older sister, and longed for the affection of a mother. He developed a crush on a woman twice his age, and although she tried to throw attractive young women in his way, he insisted upon marrying her. He walked out on her within a year. In such cases, the older woman should recognize the infatuation for what it is and ward off the ardent swain gently but firmly.

Crushes of a girl or boy for another youngster of the same sex are common at this stage. Two girls may be inseparable. They may hug and kiss and be jealously possessive. They share secrets and plan good times together. In this way they satisfy a desire for affection. Others may scorn this crush because it seems to carry connotations of sexual relations. In any event, the crush usually ends when one girl gets a boy friend. Similarly, two boys who find a deep satisfaction in the company of each other may be inseparable. Usually, there is no sexual feeling between them. They eventually drift apart, but remain friends.

The danger of homosexuality arises when a crush between two girls or two boys lasts. The person who succumbs to this practice is usually a chronic masturbator, and frequently his homosexuality can be traced back to improper sex education. The weaker partner of the homosexual pair is usually one who responds to a love which has been denied by his parents.

Once she begins dating, the adolescent girl may fall "in love with love." The thrill she feels when in the arms of a boy is the thrill of being admired, which she might feel regardless of the specific boy involved. She is not concerned with sex; her partner is a dream prince, a symbol of the man she will marry when she meets him. The boy too may not be thinking of this particular girl he is embracing; he may be dreaming of the wife and children he will have some day. Thus, both boy and girl may simulate a love unrelated to the partner of the moment.

If the boy has had sex experiences, he may suddenly attempt to make violent love. The girl, awakened from her daydream, may be frightened and repelled and jerk herself away. She may be extremely angry if the boy explains that he was "just trying her out," and ashamed that he thought her that kind of girl. If she is ignorant of sex matters, she may not know what is happening until it is too late. On the other hand, the boy may recognize her ignorance and control himself before conditions get out of hand.

"Going steady" is an adolescent fad which parents often dislike but can usually break up if they wish. The girl has a constant escort to take her out. The boy usually enjoys the freedom of her home, stays to meals, and raids the refrigerator at will. Of course, there are dangers: a close attachment tends to breed sexual familiarity. Fortunately, in most cases the attachment rarely lasts; someone more attractive comes along.

Parents should proceed cautiously in discouraging steady dating. If you show direct opposition to your daughter's "steady," you may hurt her self-esteem and stimulate in her a loyalty to him, whether he is worthy of it or not. It is better to let her learn about the boy gradually and with your tactful assistance. If an engagement seems imminent, and you think the marriage will be unfortunate and unhappy, you may have to act drastically to prevent it by sending her away to school, particularly a coeducational school, where she will meet other boys and forget the one left behind. Steady company keeping is not the proper thing except as a preparation for a possible marriage.

If your daughter has been adequately informed regarding sex and its demands, and has grown up with a belief in an all-seeing God who loves and protects her, she will not want to offend Him. On the other hand, education which has been entirely divorced from religious motives and principles and has been given in an entirely secular atmosphere may not instill a true respect for sex and its needs and limitations. When sex offenses are held as sins against God, a strong bulwark against temptation is established.

It is helpful when training in sex can be given by a teacher who is able to talk about it as a normal function. Some parents are unable to do this properly; they should seek assistance from another understanding adult, a clergyman, teacher, or doctor. Instruction which is not calm and intelligent frequently causes frigidity and impotence: a girl may be frightened into thinking that every gesture of affection has a hidden sexual desire, may suspect every boy friend, and finally enter marriage terrified. She may go home to her mother soon after marriage, disgusted with her husband's normal desires. She may remain a frigid wife, regarding her husband's love-making as repugnant no matter how much she loves him. Or she may accept her cross like a martyr and bear his children.

The boy who has not been intelligently instructed may dread marriage because his mother has warned him to beware of females seeking a husband and support. He may suspect every girl who smiles at him and therefore may refuse to let himself become involved. If he marries a girl who attracts him, he may find himself impotent because he has been taught that sex relations are dirty. Or if he has premarital relations, he may run away if the girl becomes pregnant.

Sexual Perversion

Parents should not blind themselves to the fact that sexual perverts are on the prowl. Their victims are often very young children.

Exhibitionists—those who show their private parts in public —are rarely dangerous because this act in itself relieves the sexual tension, but at any rate, you should teach your children to report every suspicious act of this kind to you. They should not be needlessly frightened and made nervous, however they should be warned against accepting candy, money, rides, or other favors from strangers. They should not go into the woods without an adult they know very well, nor go across wooded lots, nor be out at night alone.

Deliberate seduction and rape of girls occur frequently, as any reader of newspapers can testify. This is a very real danger of which daughters must be warned. However much the independent adolescent girl may object she should not be allowed to come home alone at night. If the reason for the caution is impressed upon her sufficiently, she will not rebel just because she "is sick of being told what to do." She should refuse to go on blind dates unless she has entire confidence in the girl who arranges the date for her, and she should not allow the other couple to desert her and her escort. You may say that you wish to keep your daughter happy and free from fear; unfortunately, unless you warn her of these dangers, you do not prepare her for the realities of modern life. Warnings against sex attacks can be as life saving as warnings against fires.

Such crimes against boys are also serious. Little boys are often led away and attacked by adults, and lascivious women sometimes entice teen-agers. A homosexual boy who has been initiated into abnormal practices entices other boys. He may satisfy himself with one younger, willing victim, or he may attack many boys.

Some adolescents become chronic tellers of dirty stories. They delude themselves into thinking that they're popular when they get a laugh. If you merely tell your youngster not to listen to dirty stories, he may think you are just a prude. You should also explain how his self-respect is lowered by listening. Those who habitually tell dirty stories are trying to relieve their own sex urges, or are trying to arouse sex feelings in the listener.

We may conclude that adolescence can be a period of great joy, but always creates problems which must be solved. The solution will depend upon how well prepared the youth is to adjust to unexpected changes, disappointments, and frustrations.

As we have seen, the greatest factor in successful rearing is parental love. It is true that many adolescents rise above their deprivations, somehow conquer their frustrations and go on to become admirable adults. But you should not complacently expect this to happen in your home; otherwise, delinquency can become even more alarming than it is today.

CHAPTER EIGHT

The Maladjusted Child

By no means do all spoiled or neglected children grow up maladjusted. Many emerge from their turbulent adolescence as entirely normal, well-adjusted young adults. This improvement in their behavior may be brought about because of a change in environment (adverse factors which caused their misbehavior have been eradicated) or because they have adjusted themselves to a situation which previously caused them to rebel.

Sometimes the improvement is almost unbelievable. I remember the case of Dorothy. She was fatherless, and her mother worked as a practical nurse to support her. Alone all day, Dorothy ran wild. She was noisy, destructive and deliberately used coarse language to be smart. Other children were warned not to play with her, so she tormented them in every way she could. Everyone prophesied she would come to some bad end.

Then her mother died, and Dorothy was taken to a western town by a well-to-do childless aunt. Dorothy came back to her home town when she was 19, and those who had known her when she was a child were astonished to find her a gracious, attractive young woman. When one woman remarked at the change, Dorothy laughed and replied, "Well, you can't tell by the looks of a frog how far he can jump."

A child may become maladjusted due to conditions existing both within himself and outside himself. Factors existing inside include his hereditary temperament, his intellectual powers, and his physical constitution. One child may be naturally easygoing; another, high-strung. The latter, being very active, must adjust his natural capacity for speed, whereas the easygoing child is likely to become maladjusted if he becomes involved in activities which demand rapid thinking and acting. He becomes bewildered, nervous, and resentful.

If you do not believe in hereditary temperament, stand by the window of a hospital nursery and watch the one to four-day-old infants who live under practically identical conditions. They receive the same formula, sleep in similar cribs, and enjoy the same temperature and lighting. Their diapers and clothes are changed at about the same intervals. You will notice instantly that some infants react more quickly, more violently, and more easily than others. Close the nursery door quietly: Baby Jones stirs uneasily. His neighbor, Baby Smith, sleeps on and is scarcely aroused when a bedpan clatters to the floor in the room across the hall.

Another internal factor to which a child must adjust is his intelligence level. One with superior intellect should learn to have patience with the duller thinkers, or else he may be considered a "smarty pants" or snob. Similarly, one of duller intellect should learn to function with the equipment he has; he should not be made to feel incompetent; rather, he should believe it worth while to try to improve his mind.

Each individual should also learn to adapt to his physical constitution. Height, weight, one's general state of physical health—all these factors can affect personality. A serious or prolonged illness inevitably has a psychological impact, whether the individual is six or sixty, and in the formative years the psychological effect of illness can be very great. And while the obligation of parenthood requires many virtues and much struggle even with a normal child, the task is increased many times when a child is chronically ill or suffers a severe physical handicap.

Physical Handicaps

Rheumatic Fever. The young person with a rheumatic fever may incur a residual heart disorder. He will require extensive care. Because of psychological problems resulting from the long-term invalidism which this disease makes necessary, many physicians are extremely cautious in making a diagnosis of rheumatic fever. They insist upon laboratory evidence before they order the child confined to a period of relative inactivity, which extends long after he no longer feels ill. The youngster cannot understand why he can't play and run when he feels well. He may have been frightened if he heard the doctor warn about permanent damage to his heart, but as he sees his friends playing outside, he forgets his fear and demands to be allowed to join them. As his parent, you will need all your patience to keep him contented in bed.

Diabetes. The diabetic child also should learn to adjust to his ailment. He will have to control the disease for the rest of his life. The inactivity of the child with rheumatic fever is absolutely essential. The opposite is true in the case of the diabetic child; he should resume normal activity as soon as possible. In fact, his insulin requirements are regulated according to the normal activity expected of his age. But since a delicate balance must be maintained between insulin dosage and food intake, it is absolutely necessary that his food drives be controlled. Young diabetics rebel against this standardization of food habits more than against the daily injection of one or two doses of insulin, and their tendency for rebellion should be treated along with their diabetes. Parents' patience, understanding, and utter cooperation with the physician are essential. If these children are encouraged to live as normal a life as possible, they will feel less rebellious and continue to regard themselves as part of their own crowd.

Some parents of young diabetics are overly encouraged by the recent discovery that a new drug for diabetes can be given by mouth. There is no evidence at present, however, that this new drug can replace insulin.

Obesity. Overweight is another physical abnormality which brings psychological repercussions. As in adults, in ninety to ninety-five percent of cases, the fatness is caused by overeating. Only a small percentage of obese children have a glandular disorder. A ravenous desire for food is due to a psychological disturbance. Food gives a feeling of satisfaction and a release from nervous tension. Often a child enjoys eating to excess because love is denied. Before such a child becomes obese, he no doubt has already had difficulty in his relationships with others. His unhappiness is increased when he is teased about his weight, his feeling of insecurity is intensified, and he alleviates his discomfort by eating more and more. If his parents deny his demands for food, he is convinced more than ever that he is not loved.

Recently I saw a film in which this point was illustrated perfectly. A little girl returned home from school. Her mother greeted her coldly.

"I have my report card," the child said brightly, "and I got an A in every subject but one."

The mother gave no indication of having heard. Instead, she turned to the child and spoke angrily. "I told you yesterday that I was having a bridge party this afternoon," she said. "Now don't bother me. Run upstairs and change your clothes. I don't want to be ashamed of you when my friends come."

After the guests had seated themselves around the bridge table, the girl tiptoed downstairs. To her astonishment, she overheard her mother boasting about her extraordinarily high marks. The child was completely mystified as to why the mother reacted so harshly to her and yet boasted about her to her friends. She went into the kitchen, opened the refrigerator, and took out a huge piece of cake covered with whipped cream. She ate the cake like a person on the verge of starvation. It was her substitute satisfaction for the recognition and love she had expected from her mother.

Like all habits, the habit of overeating is much easier to start than it is to stop. That is why many adults who have tried every method of weight reduction finally turn to the psychiatrist. By retracing their childhood, they may be able to establish that their obesity actually began at the age of five or so, and realize that emotional readjustments are necessary. But how much easier it would be if parents provided adequate love to begin with!

Some parents tend to encourage their children to overeat. Overprotective parents frequently urge a child to eat more food than he really needs so that he will grow big and strong. Some parents who were reared in conditions of poverty feel they must show the world that they are successful enough to feed their children properly. They regard their obese child as a symbol of their prosperity, much as others might regard a mink coat or high-powered limousine.

Parents also have a tendency to overlook the fact that children are like adults in their reactions to food. Sometimes they are very hungry; at other times they feel the need to eat little. Parents who disregard these normal variations and insist that they eat everything put before them at every meal encourage poor food habits. The child no longer eats because he is hungry, but because he is obliged to. When he reaches adulthood, and his food need grows less and less, the habit of eating everything on his plate may contribute strongly to his overweight condition.

Left-handedness. This occurs in a small percentage of children and sometimes creates psychological difficulties. Since most people are right-handed, our instruments, machines, sporting equipment, etc. are all devised for right-hand use. Right-handed persons often are not aware of their good fortune. For example, unless a left-handed person is seated at the end of the dinner table, he bumps his neighbor with his arm. Although left-handedness in itself creates problems, trying to change a left-handed person to a right-handed one usually creates greater difficulties. One frequent and serious consequence is the development of stuttering. Unless the child can be easily changed, it is better to let him remain left-handed. Of course, his left-handedness should never be ridiculed. It should be accepted in a matter-of-fact manner as a physical characteristic, like being rather short or very tall. Left-handers are often preferred in sports; a "southpaw" is eagerly awaited by each baseball team.

Polio. The crippling this disease causes gives mothers and fathers more sleepless nights than any other childhood illness. The great advances in polio vaccine have, to a great extent, alleviated the grave perils of this disease, and further advances may make it as rare as the once-dreaded diphtheria. However, polio still plays a terrifying role, and its victims suffer its scourge. The care of a polio patient in the acute stage is a matter for trained physicians and nurses. When initial stages are passed, a prolonged period of nursery care and physical therapy is often necessary. This can sometimes be handled at home.

In the case of polio, as in other childhood illnesses, parents tend to be too kind, even falsely kind. Pampering the patient after the acute phase has subsided may decrease his recovery proportionately and cause a "spoiled" disposition. It is more important to encourage children to fight their illness bravely. This can be done if the problem of crippling is faced realistically by both the parents and the children. Parents should appeal to the natural qualities of childhood—enthusiasm, energy, vitality. These are the greatest weapons against the crippling residuals of polio. If they are lacking, no doctors or physical therapists can force the recovery of lost functions.

A child spoiled before polio strikes may remain a problem child after he recovers from the disease. Little Ellen was a pretty, affectionate girl, but her mother could not bear to see the child denied a wish. When Ellen contracted polio, her mother was badly frightened and lavished even more love on the little one. During the recovery period, mother sat by her side, playing games, reading to her, catering to her every demand. When out at play again, Ellen was uncontrollable. She screamed and fought when other children refused to let her have her own way. Finally, her mother took her to a psychiatric clinic. When asked afterward what the doctor said, the mother replied frankly, "He said not to bring Ellen back again, but I should come for treatments." The same advice might well be given other parents who overprotect their once ill children.

Skin Disorders. Blemishes of some kind are common in children. Sometimes they are infectious, but more frequently they are indications that the child is allergic to a particular food or material. In either case, they should not be ignored but should be treated by a physician. Usually, the physical importance of these blemishes is slight, but their psychological importance is almost always serious.

The most psychologically disturbing skin disease is acne. It is characterized by numerous pimples and blemishes on the face, and sometimes extends to the chest and back. Acne occurs most often between adolescence and adulthood and only sometimes in preadolescence or adult years. When untreated, it can result in permanent scars—scars not only on the face, but also on the personality. A pimply face can force the shamed child into an abnormal introversion that is not easily overcome. A nine-year-old girl who attended a large party refused to thank her hostess for a good time. "I didn't have a good time," she declared. Pressed for a reason, she said that she had been left out of the charades. Another child said, with the brutal frankness characteristic of the young, "Pimply girls don't look pretty." The afflicted child may recall that incident all her life.

Parents should not ignore the problem of pimples by simply saying that they will soon be outgrown, although that is usually the case. They will deepen their relationship with the child by showing that they understand the importance of the disfigurement to the youngster and take him to a doctor for treatment.

Other Physical Handicaps. Deafness, poor eyesight or even blindness, and deformities of limbs bring special and individual problems to the child victim. One general principle of treatment can be applied: the handicap should never be increased or exaggerated by overemphasis upon its importance. The child should be treated as a normal youngster, with only necessary allowances made for his handicap.

How difficult the adjustment will be depends upon the degree of the illness or handicap. For example, eplilepsy requires many great social and economic adjustments. Most epileptic children are unaware of their actions during their attacks: when other children tell them, the afflicted ones begin to live in fear of the next seizure. Epileptics should become convinced that they can live normal lives, for many are entirely normal in intelligence and some are unusually bright. Unfortunately, they should also learn to deal with prejudice, just as many other persons are forced to deal with prejudice against their race, color, or religion. A child who cannot cope with prejudice of any kind may become revengeful and bitter.

Inasmuch as the epileptic usually has a physical warning of an attack just before it comes, he should be taught to lie on the floor before he passes out. When a convulsion occurs he should not be ashamed; rather, he should congratulate himself because this indicates that his attacks are getting further apart. Fortunately, a large percentage of epilepsy can be adequately controlled by the use of modern drugs. And a large percentage of childhood epilepsy is outgrown.

Cerebral palsy is one of the commonest causes of permanent handicap. Impairment may vary from complete spasticity of the limbs and severe mental retardation to only a slight disturbance in motor or mental functioning. Special schools and training programs have been set up to train spastic children, and the results often seem almost miraculous. Even though careful, painstaking education enables them to use their powers fully within certain limits, victims of cerebral palsy suffer intensely because of their handicap.

Cerebral palsy accounts for a large portion of mentally retarded children. Other causes of mental retardation include Mongolism, cerebral agenisis, cerebral anoxia, etc. A retarded child places an exceptional burden on parents, since he can make only a limited adjustment by himself. These children are frequently placed in institutions for permanent care. Whether or not institutional care should be given cannot be fully discussed here. Each case must be individualized, for there is no standard answer. Those who advocate institutional care in all cases are as wrong as those who advocate home care in all cases.

The factors which must be weighed in each case include the age of the parents, the presence or absence of other children, the socio-economic status of the family, the emotional stability of the family group, their philosophy of life, etc. Some devoted parents would not even consider placing their child in an institution. Others obviously lack the marital or emotional stability to accept and integrate such children into their home. Between these two extremes is every kind of situation. Physicians, clergymen, professional people generally, as well as relatives and friends, should not force their own opinions on distraught parents. They should acquaint the parents with the facts involved, but the parents themselves should make the difficult decisions.

Relatives may insist that a family follow a certain course

of action, but it is the family that must live with the decision. I recall the case of Bruce. He was a smiling, sweet-faced child of kindly, respectable parents of the lower middle class. He was an idiot. His head was overly large, his body short and squatty, and he was able to move only his lower arms and hands. He shook rattles and other playthings with delight and could make his demands known by loud yells, or by thumping his toys against his bed.

Bruce's retarded condition became evident before he was a year old, and the parents considered putting him in an institution. But their relatives objected fiercely and finally the family was persuaded to care for him at home. Many of the chores of caring for him fell upon Louise, a normal, polite child, who, like her mother, was pale and thin. She seldom got out to play during her childhood because she had to help her mother. When she was eighteen, and her brother twenty, she consented to marry a young man if he would live near her mother so that when he was at work, she could run over and help. When her husband was transferred out of town, she refused to go with him: she had to help care for Bruce, who had grown so heavy that it took all three of the family to lift him off the bed to put on clean bedding. Her marriage failed, and the entire life of the family was spent caring for this adult-sized baby—all due to the insistence of relatives, who continued to live normal lives.

Psychosomatic Illnesses

Many children are handicapped by less debilitating illnesses known as psychosomatic disorders—that is, both physical and mental. One of the most important of these is asthma. A surprising number of children are now being treated by allergy clinics and by private allergists throughout the country, and emergency rooms of our hospitals have frequent visits from children with asthmatic crises, which are very frightening to the parents.

The importance of psychological factors in both the cause and the treatment of asthma must be recognized. Often a direct association can be found between the individual asthmatic attack and some psychologically important incident. For instance, a young asthmatic in the pediatric ward of a large hospital developed a strange pattern of attacks. His father visited him regularly. Then, an hour or two after the father departed, a new asthmatic attack began. Doctors studying his case concluded that like many asthmatics, the boy was polite and well controlled on the surface but teemed with hostility underneath. Secretly, he resented his father but was afraid to express it openly. In another case, the mother of a little girl noted that she had a bad attack every Wednesday when a test in spelling was scheduled.

An asthma attack is extremely distressing. It may be relieved by use of bronchodilator drugs. But, these agents relieve only symptoms. Psychotherapy must be used, not to get the individual to adjust to his illness, as in the case of an incurable disease, but to get him to adjust better to his family, his home life, his school life, or to any other sources of his emotional disturbance.

Other psychosomatic illnesses of children include many skin eruptions such as hives, digestive upsets, and cardiovascular disturbances, which may result in fainting attacks. In these illnesses, psychotherapy is the principal mode of treatment, with medications given for the bodily symptoms. For example, skin lesions may be helped by the use of various ointments, ultra-violet light, etc.

Social Maladjustments

Besides adjustments which a child must make in relation to his mental and physical abilities and handicaps, he must also adjust to the world about him—to his parents, home life, neighborhood, and school. Of these, family adjustment is the most important. As I pointed out earlier, one of the greatest problems a child may face is the feeling of being unwanted by his parents. From the time of his conception, he may be regarded as an intruder. This feeling is not uncommon, although most parents try to cover up such feelings. Children born to such unwilling parents are almost certain to suffer psychological hurt as a result of parental hostility and basic rejection.

Adopted children often have a far better psychological background than children unwanted by their natural parents. Of course, much depends upon the reasons for their adoption and the type of home they are given. There are few subaverage homes, for the adoption agencies prevent unworthy foster parents from adopting youngsters they could not or would not properly care for. Whether the children learn of their adoption and how they are told will affect their attitude toward their new parents. If the parents do not tell the child the truth at an early age, he may be terribly hurt if he discovers it later. He may discount the love of his adopted parents and resent them. He may have delusions about his natural parents, thinking they were very fine people; or, he may fear that they were very evil.

Evelyn was a happy child and became a happy woman. As a child, she was told that she had been adopted. Her parents often told her how she had been left in a railroad station by, it was thought, someone who had kidnapped her; they always assured her that they had selected her from many others at the adoption service because they fell in love with her immediately. When Evelyn grew up, she remarked that her own parents could have been no better than her adopted ones and they might not have been half as nice.

The question of having been adopted occurs commonly among children, especially if they are unhappy at home or feel unloved. This is called the "myth of adoption." The youngster believes that any mistreatment he receives is due to the fact that the adult is not his real parent but only pretends to be.

Illegitimate children present a different and more serious problem. That he may be illegitimate does not occur to the average child because he does not know that such a problem exists. However, during adolescence the question may arise, especially if he sees his parents' wedding certificate or his own birth certificate. It is generally unwise for parents to reveal illegitimacy to their children, unless they have reasonable evidence that the child suspects his status. If this is true, then they should discuss the facts openly and frankly with the child. They can mention their regrets as a result of their behavior, but they should not fail to emphasize their joy over his birth and the fact that having him made up for their sorrow.

Stepchildren have their own particular problems. They may find it impossible to compete with half sisters and brothers or stepbrothers and sisters for the affection of their stepparent. Fortunately, this is not always true, despite the fairy tales which tell of the mean stepparent and the poor little stepchild.

A child's maladjustment may arise from family discord. Quarrels between brothers and sisters are natural and should be expected. In fact, the spats are even necessary to help the children learn to get along with other human beings. These quarrels are not the same, however, as rivalry or jealousy among the children for parental affection. Such rivalry ultimately can cause serious personality defects: this rivalry occurs less in large families than in those with two or three children. Maladjustment is not apt to develop in a family closely knit by common interests and shared experiences, where brothers and sisters appreciate their parents and each other and are tied together with bonds of affection and companionship.

Fighting between parents is serious, however. This discord works untold hardship on the children. As we have stressed, young persons must feel secure in order to develop strong personalities; if their home life is shattered by quarrels or other evidence of lack of love between parents, their personalities may not develop normally and may be scarred for life. The ultimate in parental discord is the divorce court and a broken home. And statistics are emphatic in revealing the relationship between broken homes and juvenile delinquency, emotional inadequacy, and eventual adult criminality.

A home broken by divorce is far more tragic than one broken by death, because the unhappy atmosphere preceding the divorce causes havoc in the child's personality development. Whatever the cause, the absence of one parent can create a difficult situation for the child. It has been said that a youngster is like a small plant that needs supporting sticks, one on each side, to grow straight and tall. If one support is absent, the plant lacks a guide for correct growth. One remaining parent can never fully compensate for the absence of the other figure. Therefore, it helps the child if a kind uncle or another man takes, to some degree at least, the place of a dead or absent father. Likewise, a grand-mother or aunt can give some support by taking the role of a dead mother. Through such substitutions, the child can have both a mother and a father figure to whom he can relate his experience of living.

Parents who quarrel, bicker, or drink to excess do more than hurt the personality development of their children. They give youngsters a distorted outlook on life which may ulti-mately lead to equally degraded behavior.

Parents who drink too much endanger their children's standards of morality. Not only do children imitate their lax parents, but other persons look down upon the offspring and may even tell them that they can come to no good, as though wickedness is inherited.

The bond that exists between parents and child is the most important factor in developing the youngster's ability to adjust. It is because of this strong parent-child bond that many children emerge well-adjusted from what seem to be grossly inadequate homes. And the lack of this bond is a cause for many maladjusted children who come from ap-parently ideal homes. The parent-child relationship is more important than anything else—the food the child eats, his clothes, his school, his playmates.

As proof, consider the case of Mr. R. He regarded himself as a very devout man. He was extremely critical of what he considered wrongdoing. His son, Robert, was as strong-willed as himself. At first Robert tried to please his father but soon became discouraged because even his most innocent act was "bad" in the father's eyes. Usually Robert was not whipped for these acts; instead, he was forced to get on his knees and beg God's forgiveness. If little boys came to play with him, they too were urged to get down and pray. Continually in fear of his father, Robert did badly at school and was up-braided by his teachers. He became a frequent truant. Finally, when Robert was fifteen, his father threatened to have him committed to an institution, something he really would not have done, for this religious zealot was continually praying for his wayward son. One day the boy disappeared and never came back. This was a home that had everything—everything, that is, but a good father-son relationship.

Some parents seem to think that their function is finished when the child is born. One would be shocked to learn of the many ways in which infants are neglected. Some parents never take their children to a physician, even when they are seriously ill, not because of financial reasons, but because of sheer disinterest. Some little children are inadequately clothed, not because parents lack money, but because they lack concern. Anemia or rickets due to improper feeding are not unusual diagnoses when a child is admitted to a pediatric ward of a hospital. These little ones are not always the off-spring of the poor; they come from all social and economic classes.

Even more prevalent than the physical neglect of children is psychological neglect. Many parents are really not interested in the type of school their children attend nor in how well they get along at school. They do not care to inform themselves about the companions their children associate with or their type of recreation. Providing there is no correction, guidance, or discipline, such parents may pave the road to juvenile delinquency.

Society feels that parents have basic obligations toward their offspring. Therefore, to combat guilt feelings over neglecting their children, some parents overcompensate in other ways, such as lavishing clothes and spending money on the youngsters; they must prove to the world that they care for them. Others claim to treat their children as equals, hoping to disprove the idea that basically they regard them as unimportant.

Children raised in this atmosphere are rarely fooled. They feel their parents' neglect and react to it. They develop an active hostility directed against their parents and society. If unguided, they become socially delinquent; if undisciplined, morally incorrigible.

The child can be equally maladjusted by the other extreme of parental discipline—complete dominance. Some parents exact submission from their children by wielding the rod of strict discipline. They refuse to explain why their children should behave in accordance with their demands. Coupled with this attitude of strictness come severe and frequent punishments; indeed, the two go hand in hand. One cannot have rigid and unreasoning discipline with children without enforcing the regime with harsh punishments.

Youngsters who must endure a severe home environment are no better off than the neglected or overindulged ones. They too develop a deep hostility toward society and especially toward their parents. Discipline that is reasonable and understood does not promote delinquency, because the children recognize its fairness. But discipline that is unjust and unreasoning produces adults who are hostile toward all who represent authority: to them, law and order means harshness and injustice. Therefore, overly strict training does not educate children to be good citizens, for, like complete neglect, it fosters opposition to the norms and laws designed to protect society.

Overprotective parents cripple the child's personality by trying to shelter him from harm. They are busy day and night trying to make the road of life easy. But in return, they demand that their children walk the road their way. Paradoxically, overprotective parents think they make everything easy for their children: actually, they make everything difficult. This possessive parent feels guilty because secretly— perhaps not even aware of this himself—he rejects his children. These guilt feelings drive him to pretend a loving care for the children: he rationalizes himself into believing he will never be able to do enough. Unable to rid himself of these guilt feelings, he indulges in oversolicitous care. In return, his basic selfishness demands some return for "all that he has done for his children." His constant demands for gratitude produce feelings of guilt in the offspring. Actually, this parent has given only material things; he has not given the most important thing for his child's best development —love.

Some parents who are frustrated in their own lives, or feel insecure in their accomplishments, try to relive their lives in their children. They try to prevent their children from making the same errors. They may have a real affection for their children yet nevertheless reject them as individuals. By that I mean that they do not give their children the right to live their own lives; they try to incorporate the youngsters into their own life.

These parents can be very strict. They remember their own weaknesses when they were young and they are afraid that their children will exhibit the same or different laxness. Feeling guilty about errors of their own youth, they are determined to rectify their wrongs by keeping their children from wrongdoing. Rather than enforcing normal restrictions, they insist upon behavior much stricter than that required by social and moral standards. Again, the result is hostility in their children, who are certain to resent such interference in their lives.

What happens to a child completely dominated by his parents? One of three things: he will rebel and strike out for himself; he will express his frustration in unacceptable ways; or, he will acquiesce and grow up dependent, unable to assume responsibility or make any decisions of his own. He is like the little child who does not get up when he stumbles. Instead, he yells for his mother. She rushes to pick him up, kisses the part that hurts, and spanks the object that got in his way. This child will always wait for someone to rescue him. He never learns through his own mistakes, for he doesn't think he makes any. He believes that his accidents are due to someone's meanness, or just bad luck.

Another external factor to which the developing child must adjust, namely, the socio-economic level of the home and neighborhood, has been discussed previously. This level, although less important than the psychological environment of the home itself, can cause various problems for those children coming from poor homes and neighborhoods. For instance, they are often limited in their means of recreation because they have neither the equipment nor space to enjoy games. And their natural yearning for excitement cannot be fully satisfied by family trips or outdoor jaunts. Therefore, they may stand on busy street corners or play in alleys and devise ways of obtaining thrills by "daring" the law. Such children profit from the guidance of a "big brother"—a young adult who takes the responsibility of directing a particular underprivileged boy in proper ways of conduct, showing a kindly interest in his difficulties and welfare and in his development as a person. In most cases there is a heartwarming response from those to whom kindness has been shown.

Some boys who have grown up neglected and unloved and who are defiant in their attitude toward the law, often break down when shown an unexpected kindness. Mike was always in trouble of some kind, and was sentenced to six months in jail just as a draft board called him into service. A clerk on the board asked if the boy was willing to serve in the Army if his sentence was remitted. The boy eagerly agreed. A number of boys from one community were leaving with that lot of draftees, and the clerk asked a neighborhood women's organization, which prepared knitted articles for these boys, if it could provide a sweater for Mike also. The women's group provided a complete outfit of knitted articles for him, and a son of one of the women said that when he handed the bundle to Mike at the railroad station, Mike opened it and burst into tears. He said, "No one ever gave me a present before." No matter how hard-boiled he had pretended to be, Mike needed a friend.

In good neighborhoods, one sometimes sees poor homes. Children from these homes have a different problem. Their age mates may pass remarks about their "funny" clothes, and while these remarks are not meant to be cruel, they are definitely directed against poverty and they hurt. If children have no party dress or good suit, they may be unable to attend functions which are of major importance to them. Their social life may be handicapped in similar ways: they cannot have visitors or parties, because their home is too poor for others to see, and their parents cannot afford food for guests.

Poor youngsters can be trained by their parents so that their poverty need be no handicap. They should be taught respect for poverty. They should learn the honest values of life and how to use them in their dealings with their fellow men. They should learn that having self-respect is more important than having money. The poverty of home or neighborhood, instead of being a handicap to these children, can therefore teach them the virtues of life.

Since juvenile delinquency is not necessarily the product of poor homes and neighborhoods, it follows that many problem children are from well-to-do homes and rather wealthy neighborhoods. These children are often so pampered and given so much that life is unchallenging. They expect life to continue being easy. They have little to gain by hard work since they are used to getting everything for nothing. Money can be a handicap to them unless their parents train them to have a healthy respect for work as well as for money.

Character training is one thing money can't buy; and well-to-do parents should remember this. Their wealth need be no handicap if they make an effort to keep it from being so. But, unfortunately, wealthy parents often are so busy making money and enjoying it that they give little time and attention to their children. By giving things material to their children, they think they are compensating for their own absence. The idea of devoting extra effort to give their children a proper attitude toward wealth and work does not occur to them.

A growing child or youth who is emotionally disturbed by any of these factors I have mentioned, such as a physical handicap, poor home life, parental neglect, or poor environment, may well be susceptible to the evil influence of bad companions. Dissatisfied with his own environment or with himself, he will seek security and satisfaction in something else, perhaps finding both in the companionship of others who are also insecure. Then he may be forced psychologically to follow them in their misdemeanors or crimes because it would increase his insecurity not to do so.

Parents who have won the respect and confidence of their children and who understand their problems need not fear the danger of bad companionship. These parents, who do not experience a sense of panic every time their child brings home a new playmate or finds a new friend, have confidence in their child and in the training they have given him.

Naturally, you would not want your child to associate with hoodlums. But parents who doubt their own abilities tend to be overcautious regarding their children's companions. They worry that they have not given their children the right type of home with adequate affection and instruction: consciously, or perhaps only vaguely, they realize this neglect and suspect that it creates a handicap for their youngsters. They recognize that their children's unstable position results from an insecure and incomplete background. Thus, each new companion seems to present the hazard of leading their child astray.

An obvious result springs from such parental attitudes. The children recognize that it is almost impossible to acquire friends who meet all parental demands, and they soon regard their parents as totally unreasonable. Then they may feel entirely justified in choosing companions in defiance of their elders. Thus, the parents push them into the very position they were trying so hard to prevent.

The school is second only to the family group in training the child in social consciousness. It too can be a source of maladjustment. For instance, when academic achievement is the school's only concern, it may create the feeling that only those who excel in their studies have something to contribute to society. Too frequently the classroom is a field of favorites: the chosen ones are called upon to do little tasks for the teacher or display the excellence of the class, the teacher, and the school by their recitations when visitors are to be impressed. I have observed that the more inadequate and insecure the teacher, the more she will exalt herself by showing off her better students and ignoring the poorer ones. Because of such practices, less gifted students come to feel they are just bystanders of society, of no importance in community activities. A child unfavorably compared with another child becomes frustrated by the lack of appreciation of his own worth, which he also begins to doubt.

Youngsters who cannot keep up in school with others of

their age may develop an emotional strain and a defeatist attitude unless they are placed in special classes or special schools, where they can be among those of their own intellectual level. Those who have a special difficulty in one or two subjects also may feel inferior unless assisted by remedial teaching. A frequent difficulty is in reading; the child may go on from grade to grade without ever having acquired the basic skills. He remains continually handicapped. In each grade, he finds it increasingly difficult to keep up with his classmates because his inadequate reading ability makes other subjects more and more difficult. When children are given remedial reading instruction, their other school marks often improve remarkably.

Thus, a vast number of hereditary and environmental influences help shape the child's personality. We cannot emphasize too strongly that home, school and neighborhood are important in the development of personality and each can be a cause of maladjustment. Towering above all other influences is the home.

Sometimes, as a parent, you may feel that you face an impossible job. Remember then that most children survive the problems of adjustment. The finished product in most cases *is not* a maladjusted adult. Even a child who has been treated badly may overcome his personality scars, which, while often quite apparent, are not incapacitating.

CHAPTER NINE

How Psychiatry Helps the Maladjusted

Types of Children Who Need Treatment

Most behavioral problems which you, as a parent, will be required to face will be normal problems. You may have moments of distress and difficulty as you try to guide your child into acceptable paths of behavior, and sometimes you may feel a deep sense of despair. Every parent has such moments. But the problems that produce this reaction usually can be solved by application of your own good judgment. The probability is that you will never need the aid of a psychiatrist to help in your child's upbringing.

In certain cases of maladjustment, however, psychiatric therapy is definitely indicated. In such instances, behavioral problems have gone beyond the normal range into the abnormal. These are the cases which have gotten out of hand for one reason or another and can no longer be handled by the parent, teacher, or other adult responsible for the child in question.

A typical maladjustment which may require the aid of an experienced psychiatrist, preferably with spiritual and religious beliefs, is that which results from a child's physical handicaps (see Chapter Six). Often we encounter children who require, not only medical management of the handicaps or chronic illness, but also a sympathetic understanding of their emotional reactions to these handicaps and aid in adjusting mentally to their illness and their limited environment. Such adjustment does not come easy.

Other children who may require psychiatric care include: *Unguided, undisciplined, or cruelly disciplined children.*

They can easily become incorrigible and hostile to law and order because they associate law with harshness and injustice, with oppression, not protection.

The child of the overpossessive or overprotective parent. These parents simulate tender care for their child because of feeling guilty about not wanting the child or having themselves transgressed a moral or social law. Their overconcern for the child's welfare makes them demand eternal gratitude and obedience in return. Some parents lavishly indulge their child and try to force him into a particular profession or business, regardless of the child's own aptitudes and ambitions. Either he rebels, or he obeys and never enjoys the fullness of life. In either case, he may develop serious personality disorders.

The child who is maladjusted because of an inadequate home or bad environment. Such a youngster may become socially adjusted through the interest of a capable, understanding teacher, who inspires him to develop a proper goal in preparation for a well-adjusted adulthood. Another aid may be that of the psychiatrist. The personality scars such a youngster bears after his treatment often make him more tolerant of the miseries of others and contribute to his character building.

When we treat behavioral disorders in children, we try to do two things: seek the causes which led to the maladjustment, and then remove or remedy the disturbing elements. We explore the various factors which cause the child to be unhappy and misbehave. We try to prevent or abolish such disturbances as far as possible, and if they cannot be changed, we try to make them harmless. Just as we treat bodies of water with chemicals to prevent mosquitoes from breeding, or give children shots to prevent polio, so we treat a child's environment to prevent maladjustment and delinquency. Even children who live in a poor environment are capable of rising above emotional disturbances that may poison their personalities. We teach them to think, feel, and behave in normal ways so that they will not grow up at war with society.

By poor or bad environment, we mean more than poor neighborhoods, more than evil companions, and more than impoverished homes with drunken or immoral parents. As explained earlier, maladjustment can be produced in the wealthiest home, where a child has every physical comfort. If he is deprived of what he needs most for his normal development—the feeling of being a wanted member of the family and of enjoying a protecting love—he may be continually frustrated and grieved. Or, at the other extreme, he may be smothered in a love which permits no independence, no self-expression, and no chance to grow up believing in his own strength and ability. He may suffer from overdiscipline and become resentful, aggressive, and deliberately hard to manage. Or, he may have little or no discipline; learning no control over his emotions, he may become selfish, disobedient, defiant.

Now I plan to discuss the treatment of the maladjusted child. The young child's emotional life is all important; most of the mental conflicts of adults can be traced to childhood. Since symptoms of maladjustment are recognizable in early childhood, this is when treatment is most successful.

With psychiatric treatment, we aim to cure emotional or mental disorders. If that is not entirely possible, we make an earnest effort to at least improve those who suffer from such conditions. Like treatments for physical diseases, psychiatric treatment has its limitations. For example, we know that some heart conditions are curable; others, however, can merely be improved or kept under control by constant use of proper drugs. We accept the fact that diabetes is a disease for which there is as yet no cure, but that it can be controlled. Pneumonia, on the other hand, is usually curable under modern conditions. Tuberculosis lies between these two; most cases can be controlled (or arrested), while others resist all treatments. Even in cured cases, however, the disease leaves scars in the lungs and may recur, so that constant precautions must be taken. Skin cancer is curable because it is visible and can be treated early, but some internal cancers may not be recognized in time to be cured.

Different Kinds of Treatment

Different types of mental disease resemble various bodily diseases in respect to their curability and incurability. Most mental disturbances can be cured, particularly if treated early; others resist all forms of treatment because they have progressed too far. Even patients who have been cured of mental disorders may show little quirks of character, which are scars of their illness; and some are susceptible to new mental upsets.

Modern methods of psychiatric treatment may be considered from the viewpoint of how they affect the patient, either physically or mentally. Physical methods include hydrotherapy (water baths), electro-shock or convulsive therapy, and lobotomy (brain surgery). In addition, many wonderworking drugs are available to the physician. Mental treatments (psychotherapy) are a healing of the mind. They include personal interviews, counseling, persuasion, reassurance, psychoanalysis, hypnosis, play therapy, and many other techniques known to the modern psychiatrist.

Like medical treatment, psychiatric treatment may also be considered symptomatic and etiological. Symptomatic treatment merely relieves symptoms and makes no attempt to get at their cause. It is like treating tuberculosis with cough syrup—the cough is relieved but the disease goes on unchecked. Tranquilizing or "happy" drugs indicate symptomatic treatment when they are used alone without psychotherapy.

Etiological treatment searches for basic causes which produce the symptoms. It deals with the environmental factors which affect the child, such as the social standing of the parents, the kind of community in which they live, their church affiliation, etc. It considers the influence of broken homes and their dire effect upon child rearing. It considers every aspect of living which may have an effect upon the child's development. Etiology offers more complete therapy than the child would obtain elsewhere—for these reasons:

When a youngster has a stomachache, constipation, or

headache, he is taken by his parents to a physician in order to discover what caused the disorder. When a child does poorly in school, parents may discuss the fact with his teacher, and perhaps the teacher has already thought of seeking aid from the school psychologist. Parents who are worried about their child's misbehavior may talk to a clergyman, who can question the lad regarding his moral and religious attitude. Or parents dissatisfied with their home life may seek advice from a social worker, who examines the environment of the family.

All these specialists have training and skill in particular fields. All seek to help the child become better equipped for life. But while each specialist knows a particular way in which he can contribute, he knows little of the contributions of other specialists. The parents may not tell the physician that Tom is a poor pupil; they may not tell his teacher that Tom has headaches consistently. The physician may not realize Tom has problems at home and school. And the clergyman may not know that Tom's behavior is a direct result of the parents' lack of harmony. On the other hand, a psychiatrist tries to determine whether the boy is upset by disturbances in the home and family and whether a physical handicap causes the difficulty at school. He will study, not only Tom's physical health, but also his emotional life is its particular environment. Thus, the psychiatrist gets the complete story.

In child guidance centers, psychologists, psychiatric social workers, nurses, and psychiatrists work closely together. They know what each specialist is doing and have consultations together about the child. All factors bearing on the problem—physical, religious, emotional, environmental—are weighed; together they present a clear picture of the trouble and make possible a well-founded plan for treatment. A parent of an emotionally disturbed child wants him cured quickly, as does the physician. But these cases often take time. Since they usually do not develop overnight, they cannot be cleared up overnight. First we must determine what is really wrong —what underlies the emotional upset.

How We Treat a Child

Let us consider the case of a child brought to the clinic because of his temper tantrums and frightening nightmares. The parents merely want him to sleep all night through so that he will not disturb their own sleep. And they want him to obey their commands blindly—none of these temper tantrums. Just like that! All that the doctor must do, they imply, is adjust a screw or two and change the youngster into a trouble-free machine. Alas, human nature is not that simple. For the emotional disturbance at the root of this sleeplessness is not caused by one stress or one single conflict: it results from a combination of some of the factors we discussed earlier.

Let us begin the treatment by examining the history of the child—the story of his life and everything related to him. One or both parents should come, without the child, for the history interview. If the child is present, neither doctor nor parent can freely discuss his problem. And if the little one sits for an hour in the waiting room while doctor and parent discuss him, he may become frightened as he wonders what terrible things they are preparing for him.

At the initial interview, the parent is led to tell everything about the child and his symptoms. This is not difficult, since the parent is anxious about the unhappy youngster. The interviewer does not interrupt while the parent is talking, except possibly with some question regarding a date or a particular occurrence. When the parent has finished, the doctor asks questions to clarify points which have not been covered. This history is recorded chronologically (year by year) and includes a description of each symptom.

At first, the parent may describe only one or two symptoms, thinking they are the child's only complaint. In the case we are considering, we learn from the first interview that the temper tantrums and nightmares began with no apparent cause when the child was about six years old. They continued almost uninterruptedly for four years. The boy is ashamed of his tantrums and never wants his father told about them.

In the beginning, the parents did not bother about them, thinking that they would soon stop. Then they punished him in various ways, deprived him of privileges, and spanked him —all without effect.

The boy is given a thorough physical examination; it uncovers nothing physically wrong. A study of his physical condition reveals, however, that he has been constipated since the age of six, at which time his misbehavior began.

Now there are additional interviews. We learn that in his nightmares he dreams that he is pursued by terrible men.

We note that the family considers him a "very good" child except for the tantrums. He is exceedingly obedient to his mother and rarely objects to her wishes. But he is shy with his father and apparently afraid of him. This fear started just before his symptoms began. He is also hostile toward his six-year-old brother, who, although younger, is a bigger, stronger boy.

The patient shows extreme fear of every man unless the man is accompanied by a woman. When he plays with boys, his attitude is extreme, either quite aggressive or too compliant. In school his behavior is perfect and he stands near the head of his class. During recreation time he prefers to be alone so that he can read. All in all, he appears to be a secluded child, finding satisfaction in exaggerated obedient behavior toward mother and teacher, and gratification in passing his rivals in school. His chief trouble appears to be an excessive, unreasonable fear of men.

We look closely into his very early history. He was a full-term baby, with normal birth. He was breast-fed for six months, then gradually weaned. His mother began bowel training early, and it was completed at the early age of ten months. While still a baby, he sucked his thumb, for which he was severely and promptly punished. When he was six, his mother became much upset because he fingered his genitals; she acted quickly to stop it. Every time the little one put his fingers near the middle of his body he was scolded, threatened, and slapped; yet he continued to touch his genitals for some time. Eventually, he gave in to his mother, but shortly thereafter, his temper tantrums began.

The boy's psychosexual development is summarized as follows: finger sucking, bowel and bladder pleasures, and touching the genitals (a normal series of episodes in children) were all severely curtailed. This curtailment imposed unnecessarily severe conflicts between the little child's instinctual desires and his wish to please his mother.

What injurious effects have these various experiences produced? Following them, the child developed intense feelings and strong emotional reactions which he was unable to control and about which he felt anxious and helpless: he expressed his emotional turmoil by suddenly letting go in a temper tantrum, or by having an anxiety attack such as a terrifying nightmare.

From our study of all the factors in this case, we can say that a part of this boy's trouble was caused by his mother's strictness regarding his early childhood sexual behavior. For example, at the age of six, when he masturbated, she overemphasized the act and forcibly stopped it. All his offenses made him feel insecure about her affection, which he craved.

Further interviewing of the mother reveals that she lost her first child, a girl who had lived only six months. She continually worried that she would lose her second child too. Therefore, any attempt at independent action on his part was regarded as dangerous and was checked.

When he was four years old, his mother directed most of her attention to his newly arrived sister. This change was hard to take and made the boy very unhappy. He turned his attention and love to his maternal grandfather, who unfortunately died within a few months. The child believed that his grandfather had left him deliberately because he was a "bad" boy. His father was frequently absent from home on account of business and political interests, and paid little attention to his son. As we learn of these details, we can observe that by the time he was five years old the boy blamed men for his unhappiness and feared all of them.

Now we know the roots of our patient's troubles. Because of a series of hurting experiences in the first six years of his life, this boy developed neurotic feelings, which he expressed in behavior different from that of the average child of his sex, age, and social situation. When he lost the attention he enjoyed, and it was transferred to the baby, he felt deserted and alone. Having temper tantrums was the only way he could attract attention to himself. What is the best treatment under these circumstances? It is to relieve the child of his fear and unhappiness and to make the parents aware that they should give the affection he desires and free him from rigorous restraint.

In this case, as in many behavioral cases, psychotherapy is required to restore a proper emotional outlook and help the child develop freely and properly. It aims to reëducate the child for a proper relationship with the persons surrounding him and with his environment; namely, correcting the boy's views regarding men. The most important tool for accomplishing this is a relationship between therapist and child—what we call rapport. The boy transfers his anxieties, tensions, and rebellion to the therapist. He expects to be scolded, perhaps even punished. But instead of trying to suppress such behavior, the psychiatrist skillfully guides the youngster to a new view of his own responsibility and of his relationship to others. Acceptance of this new point of view, however, arises in the child himself. Only when this occurs is he able to overcome his insecurity and tension and stop his abnormal behavior.

Though the child and the therapist start out alone in evaluating the child's role, they soon require the cooperation of others—especially his parents, the primary cause of his trouble. For unless parents are reëducated in order to assume their proper roles, simultaneous with the child's reëducation, the treatment will have little lasting effect. When they become aware of the basic problem, the parents—and also the teacher—can help an emotionally unbalanced child. Then, instead of suppressing the child's needs, which underlie the basic problem, they will provide for the proper expression and satisfaction of these needs. When the psychiatrist brings parents and teacher to recognize the causes of maladjustment, they will all be on the way to solving the child's problem.

His relationship with the therapist is a deep experience

for the child. He sees that this new person stresses certain limits of behavior, yet makes no fuss about misconduct. For the first time, the youngster meets an adult who will neither dominate nor be dominated; who accepts the boy as he is and does not try to change him into a different person. The child grows to understand himself and builds up his self-esteem; he learns with pride that he is an independent person with his own specific place and duties.

The most important single factor in helping a child who displays behavioral difficulties is the same as is used in treating a physical ailment: start treatment early, before his problem becomes acute. As we all know, serious problems usually grow out of quite mild ones. Waiting to seek help until a child is severely upset emotionally is as unreasonable as waiting until he is desperately ill with pneumonia before calling the family doctor.

Those who work with children—teachers, police, probation officers, recreation workers, clergymen, pediatricians, nurses, social workers—are in a position to note these early problems and see that they are corrected before bad habits are established. They should be familiar with the basic principles of treatment in order to help children adjust harmoniously in everyday situations.

About twenty years ago, when child guidance clinics were established in various cities of the United States, workers in the clinics made careful studies to determine the nature of each child's difficulties. But they failed to appreciate the part played by both parents and child in his social development. Now we know that the problem cannot be solved through the child alone, nor through the parents alone, but rather through the relationship existing between *parents* and *child*. In this way the treatment attains a wholesomeness and balance.

How Child Guidance Clinics Work

Let us consider the atmosphere of the clinic. In the first interview, the parents describe the child's problems and talk with a person who is obviously interested in them and in how they feel; who recognizes their hesitation and doubt as well as their willingness to do what they can to help. Their own share in the treatment is explained. The clinic's methods —separate interviews for child and parent by different staff members; the frequency and regularity of the appointments; the amount of the fee—are all discussed frankly. Then the child is brought to the clinic, and this is a strange new experience for him. The parent who brings him is seen by one staff member while the child is having a separate interview. Parent and child leave the clinic together, feeling that they have shared an experience.

The kindly understanding which the therapist shows in this early interview and the direction which his treatment takes determine, to a great extent, the outcome of the case. If the child is old enough to understand, his parents should prepare him for the first visit by explaining that they are visiting the therapist because both he and themselves may need help. The child may be anxious about what will happen —perhaps afraid, angry or defiant, perhaps indifferent. But the therapist accepts him as he is. If the patient is angry, he is allowed to give full vent to his rage. If he is scared, he finds the support of someone who understands why he feels as he does and who does not try to talk him out of that feeling too soon. The youngster who has come ready to fight finds a friend who is genuinely interested in him. Whatever the child says or does is the center of the therapist's interest, and each word or act is considered as related to the whole problem.

Unfortunately, child guidance clinics are mostly concerned with courts, family agencies, the school, and the general public, and in this way are separated from the clinical medical situation. The child psychiatrist, a medical doctor, works in his private office. He may engage, at times, a clinical psychologist or even a social worker to administer psychological tests. But often he is able to handle the problem on his own. He may see the child one hour a week and either the father or mother for an hour a week. Or, he may see the child for forty minutes and the mother for twenty minutes.

In most cases, no lengthy psychotherapeutic interviews or sessions are necessary for a successful treatment.

As the child begins to talk, he may express his feelings and state what he thinks causes them. Of course, according to him, the fault is never his. Sometimes the therapist may encourage him to talk freely; or, he may wait patiently for a response. A youngster may, in discussing his troubles, show a willingness to do something about them himself. Whatever the child does or says is influenced by the therapist's presence and willingness to listen. The youngster may talk on about his gang, his dislike of school, how good or mean each person is to him, and so on.

The child is accepted as he is, without comment or rebuke. Regardless of whether he is angry or fearful, happy or sad, aggressive or appealing, talkative or silent, the therapist is interested, because these feelings indicate the way in which the troubled child seeks to get along in his little world. The patient finds that he is accepted as having the ability to act acceptably toward others. A significant relationship is established between him and the therapist. This relationship influences the meetings that follow.

Instead of talking, the patient may plunge into play with toys chosen from among those lying around him. Whatever he says or does while playing reveals his feelings about the immediate situation. For it is not the type of play that matters, but the actions of the child toward the person trying to help him. The therapist may encourage the child to play in various ways according to the type of personality disorder, such as drawing and painting, taking part in plays, puppet shows, molding plastic materials, etc. A method used with success by one therapist may fail when used by another; but in each case, the method must be adapted to the individual child.

One of the many kinds of play therapy is finger painting, which reveals a child's natural way of expressing his feelings. The patient paints on wet paper with his bare fingers, using knuckles, fingernails, even his whole hand. This play is natural, and yet pliant; even clumsy fingers and hands can create something of interest and beauty. And once a child finds a way to express his ideas, he takes a step toward understanding himself. By recognizing his feelings and learning to control them, he begins to chart his own course. Some children present a different aspect of themselves once they embark upon finger painting. Noisy children may become completely absorbed in their painting. A quiet child may become jubilant over the effect of his creation. A nervous child may relax completely.

Finger painting is one form of "nondirective play therapy" —it allows the child to become expansive and to show depth of feeling. Such expression is encouraged by the therapist, as is revealed in his general attitude, in the interest shown on his face, in his tone of voice, and his actions. He allows the patient to explain his paintings without interruption, correction, or criticism. Thus, the child endows his creations with a meaning he wishes to express. The therapist, recognizing their true meaning, tactfully leads the child to an understanding of what he really is expressing, so that the youngster gains insight into his own behavior. Once he understands his feelings, he begins to recognize that he can gain mastery over them, rather than have them master him.

The child leads the way in this activity. The therapist makes no attempt to direct his words or actions, for probing questions will cause the youngster's confidences to stop. The therapist gives help only when the child asks for it, and makes no attempt to hurry the treatment. When the child is ready to reveal his thoughts and feelings, he will do so. Any attempt to force them out will cause retreat. The therapist's patience and understanding are therefore of prime importance.

Two world wars and their aftermaths have given all of us a realization of the existence of mental and emotional diseases. In World War II, one out of three inductees was rejected because of a mental or emotional disorder. At the end of the war, almost half of the medical discharges were due to mental and emotional disorders.

We know now that we can prevent mental disorders. The time to do so is in the early periods of life—during childhood and adolescence. These are the times when youngsters can not only find purpose in living and develop healthy attitudes toward life, but can also turn down wrong paths and develop mental attitudes that will cripple them just as surely as any physical injury.

Often the problem presented by a child may seem extremely complex. However, compared to those of adults with their fixed and rigid compulsive habits, they can generally be understood more easily because the child's experiences have been brief and simple.

In my practice of child psychiatry, I have met the psychotic, the psychoneurotic, and the maladjusted of later life. In searching for causes and backgrounds, always I have uncovered a story of neglect, mistreatment, or a complete misunderstanding of a child.

Personality maladjustments will usually *not* occur if your child's basic needs are gratified. If he feels wanted and cherished, if he is taught respect for the true values of life, he can adapt himself to the constant changes of living. Even the worst environmental evils—slum conditions, lawless companions and acquaintances—can be compensated for if you give your child proper home training in acceptable behavior and respect for moral and social laws.

A child who grows up maladjusted may be soured and embittered, suspicious of everyone, secretly despising himself. People may avoid him because he is touchy, quarrelsome, and disagreeable. Because this inability to get along with others is so noticeable, the maladjusted seem numerous indeed. Actually, however, it is an impressive and happy fact that most children survive the problems of growing up, in spite of all the odds against them, and become acceptable, respected citizens.

By applying what is known today about the psychological needs of young children, you can help your child to be a happy, normal youngster—healthy physically, spiritually, and psychologically. If you pursue your role as parent with love, kindness, and understanding, you need have no real fears of what the future will bring. For your child will have security —and therefore happiness—in his own expanding world.

ABOUT THE AUTHOR

DR. ROBERT P. ODENWALD, a practicing psychiatrist for thirty-four years, has studied extensively both abroad and in the United States. Now in private practice, he has in the past been affiliated with many public institutions and organizations. From 1948 to 1953 he was assistant professor of psychiatry at the Catholic University of America, as well as director of the University's Child Center. He has been connected with the Catholic Charities Guidance Institute and St. Vincent's Hospital, both in New York City, and was chief neuropsychiatrist at the Good Samaritan Hospital in Suffern, New York. He is a Fellow of the American Medical Association, the American Psychiatric Association, the American Medical Writers' Association, and the American Society of Group Psychotherapy and Psychodrama, American Geriatrics Association, the Association for the Advancement of Psychotherapy, A Diplomate of the American Board of Psychiatry and Neurology; and is a member of numerous medical and psychiatric societies. Dr. Odenwald is the author of many pamphlets and articles in medical, scientific and Catholic papers, and is co-author of the book PSYCHIATRY AND CATHOLICISM. He is a member of the Advisory Board of the National Academy of Religion and Mental Health, and was given the Family Catholic Action Award by the National Catholic Welfare Conference in 1952.

Image Books

... MAKING THE WORLD'S FINEST
CATHOLIC LITERATURE AVAILABLE TO ALL

OUR LADY OF FATIMA
By William Thomas Walsh
D1—75¢

THE SPIRIT OF CATHOLICISM
By Karl Adam D2—85¢

DAMIEN THE LEPER
By John Farrow D3—85¢

A POPULAR HISTORY OF THE
CATHOLIC CHURCH
By Philip Hughes D4—95¢

MR. BLUE
By Myles Connolly D5—65¢

THE DIARY OF A COUNTRY PRIEST
By Georges Bernanos D6—75¢

THE CHURCH SPEAKS TO THE
MODERN WORLD:
*The Social Teachings of Leo
XIII. Edited by Etienne Gilson*
D7—95¢

PEACE OF SOUL
By Fulton J. Sheen D8—75¢

LIFT UP YOUR HEART
By Fulton J. Sheen D9—75¢

STORM OF GLORY
*The Story of St. Thérèse of
Lisieux. By John Beevers*
D10—75¢

THE PERFECT JOY OF ST. FRANCIS
By Felix Timmermans
D11—85¢

SAINTS FOR OUR TIMES
By Theodore Maynard
D12—95¢

INTRODUCTION TO THE DEVOUT
LIFE
*By St. Francis de Sales. Newly
translated and edited by John
K. Ryan* D13—95¢

THE ROAD TO DAMASCUS
Edited by John A. O'Brien
D14—75¢

JOYCE KILMER'S ANTHOLOGY OF
CATHOLIC POETS *With a new
supplement by James Edward
Tobin* D15—$1.25

BERNADETTE AND LOURDES
By Michel de Saint-Pierre
D16—85¢

THE IMITATION OF CHRIST
By Thomas à Kempis. A Modern Version edited with an Introduction by Harold C. Gardiner, S.J. D17—75¢

THE EVERLASTING MAN
By G. K. Chesterton D18—85¢

A GRAMMAR OF ASSENT
*By John Henry Cardinal Newman with an Introduction by
Etienne Gilson* D19—95¢

A WATCH IN THE NIGHT
By Helen C. White D20—95¢

BROTHER PETROC'S RETURN
By S. M. C. D21—65¢

ST. FRANCIS OF ASSISI
By Johannes Jörgensen
D22—95¢

STORIES OF OUR CENTURY BY
CATHOLIC AUTHORS
Edited by John Gilland Brunini and Francis X. Connolly
D23—95¢

AUTOBIOGRAPHY OF A HUNTED
PRIEST
*By John Gerard. Introduction
by Graham Greene* D24—95¢

FATHER MALACHY'S MIRACLE
By Bruce Marshall D25—75¢

ON THE TRUTH OF THE CATHOLIC
FAITH *Summa Contra Gentiles Book I: God. Newly translated, with Introduction and
notes by Anton C. Pegis*
D26—95¢

6

Image Books

. . . MAKING THE WORLD'S FINEST
CATHOLIC LITERATURE AVAILABLE TO ALL

ON THE TRUTH OF THE CATHOLIC FAITH
Summa Contra Gentiles Book II: Creation. Newly translated, with an Introduction and notes by James F. Anderson D27—95¢

ON THE TRUTH OF THE CATHOLIC FAITH
Summa Contra Gentiles Book III: Providence. Newly translated, with an Introduction and notes by Vernon J. Bourke
D28a Book III, Part 1—95¢
D28b Book III, Part 2—95¢

ON THE TRUTH OF THE CATHOLIC FAITH
Summa Contra Gentiles Book IV: Salvation. Newly translated, with an Introduction and notes, By Charles J. O'Neil D29—95¢

THE WORLD'S FIRST LOVE
By Fulton J. Sheen D30—85¢

THE SIGN OF JONAS
By Thomas Merton D31—95¢

PARENTS, CHILDREN AND THE FACTS OF LIFE *By Henry V. Sattler, C.SS.R.* D32—75¢

LIGHT ON THE MOUNTAIN : The Story of La Salette
By John S. Kennedy D33—65¢

EDMUND CAMPION
By Evelyn Waugh D34—75¢

HUMBLE POWERS
By Paul Horgan D35—75¢

SAINT THOMAS AQUINAS
By G. K. Chesterton D36—75¢

APOLOGIA PRO VITA SUA
By John Henry Cardinal Newman Introduction by Philip Hughes D37—95¢

A HANDBOOK OF THE CATHOLIC FAITH
By Dr. N. G. M. Van Doornik, Rev. S. Jelsma, Rev. A. Van De Lisdonk. Ed. Rev. John Greenwood D38—$1.45

THE NEW TESTAMENT
Official Catholic edition D39—95¢

MARIA CHAPDELAINE
By Louis Hémon D40—65¢

SAINT AMONG THE HURONS
By Francis X. Talbot, S.J. D41—95¢

THE PATH TO ROME
By Hilaire Belloc D42—85¢

SORROW BUILT A BRIDGE
By Katherine Burton D43—85¢

THE WISE MAN FROM THE WEST
By Vincent Cronin D44—85¢

EXISTENCE AND THE EXISTENT
By Jacques Maritain D45—75¢

THE STORY OF THE TRAPP FAMILY SINGERS
By Maria Augusta Trapp D46—95¢

THE WORLD, THE FLESH AND FATHER SMITH
By Bruce Marshall D47—75¢

THE CHRIST OF CATHOLICISM
By Dom Aelred Graham D48—95¢

SAINT FRANCIS XAVIER
By James Brodrick, S.J. D49—95¢

SAINT FRANCIS OF ASSISI
By G. K. Chesterton D50—65¢

Image Books

*...making the world's finest
Catholic literature available to all*

VIPERS' TANGLE
by François Mauriac D51—75¢

THE MANNER IS ORDINARY
by John LaFarge, S.J. D52—95¢

MY LIFE FOR MY SHEEP
by Alfred Duggan D53—90¢

THE CHURCH AND THE RECONSTRUCTION OF THE MODERN WORLD: *The Social Encyclicals of Pius XI.* Edited by T. P. McLaughlin, C.S.B. D54—$1.25

A GILSON READER: *Selections from the Writings of Etienne Gilson.* Edited by Anton C. Pegis.
D55—95¢

THE AUTOBIOGRAPHY OF ST. THERESE OF LISIEUX: *The Story of a Soul. A new translation by* John Beevers. D56—65¢

HELENA
by Evelyn Waugh D57—65¢

THE GREATEST BIBLE STORIES
A Catholic Anthology from World Literature. Edited by Anne Fremantle. D58—75¢

THE CITY OF GOD—St. Augustine. Edited with Intro. by Vernon J. Bourke. Foreword by Etienne Gilson. D59—$1.45

SUPERSTITION CORNER
by Sheila Kaye-Smith D60—65¢

SAINTS AND OURSELVES
Ed. *by Philip Caraman, S.J.*
D61—95¢

CANA IS FOREVER
by Charles Hugo Doyle
D62—75¢

ASCENT OF MOUNT CARMEL—St. John of the Cross. Translated and Edited by E. Allison Peers.
D63—$1.25

RELIGION AND THE RISE OF WESTERN CULTURE
by Christopher Dawson
D64—85¢

PRINCE OF DARKNESS AND OTHER STORIES
by J. F. Powers D65—85¢

ST. THOMAS MORE
by E. E. Reynolds D66—95¢

JESUS AND HIS TIMES
2 Volumes D67A—95¢
by Daniel-Rops D67B—95¢

ST. BENEDICT
by Justin McCann, O.S.B.
D68—85¢

THE LITTLE FLOWERS OF ST. FRANCIS
Edited and Translated by Raphael Brown. D69—95¢

THE QUIET LIGHT
by Louis de Wohl D70—95¢

CHARACTERS OF THE REFORMATION
by Hilaire Belloc D71—85¢

THE BELIEF OF CATHOLICS
by Ronald Knox D72—75¢

FAITH AND FREEDOM
by Barbara Ward D73—95¢

GOD AND INTELLIGENCE IN MODERN PHILOSOPHY
by Fulton J. Sheen D74—$1.25

If your bookseller is unable to supply certain titles, write to Image Books, Department MIB, Garden City, New York, stating the titles you desire and enclosing the price of each book (plus 5¢ per book to cover cost of postage and handling). Prices are subject to change without notice.

Image Books

... MAKING THE WORLD'S FINEST
CATHOLIC LITERATURE AVAILABLE TO ALL

THE IDEA OF A UNIVERSITY
By John Henry Cardinal New-
man. Introduction by George N.
Shuster   D75—$1.35

PLAYED BY EAR: The Autobiography of Father Daniel A. Lord,
S.J.   D76—95¢

MY BELOVED: The Story of a
Carmelite Nun. By Mother
Catherine Thomas   D77—75¢

DARK NIGHT OF THE SOUL
By St. John of the Cross. Edited
and translated by E. Allison
Peers   D78—75¢

TERESA OF AVILA
By Marcelle Auclair. Translated
by Kathleen Pond   D79—$1.35

SAINT PETER THE APOSTLE
By William Thomas Walsh
                       D80—95¢

THE LOVE OF GOD
By Dom Aelred Graham, O.S.B.
                       D81—85¢

WOMAN OF THE PHARISEES
By François Mauriac. Translated by Gerard Hopkins
                       D82—75¢

THE PILLAR OF FIRE
By Karl Stern   D83—85¢

ORTHODOXY
By G. K. Chesterton   D84—75¢

THIS IS CATHOLICISM
By John J. Walsh   D85—$1.25

MEDIEVAL ESSAYS
By Christopher Dawson
                       D86—95¢

VESSEL OF CLAY
By Leo Trese   D87—65¢

SAINTS FOR SINNERS
By Alban Goodier, S.J.
                       D88—65¢

THE LONG LONELINESS
By Dorothy Day   D89—85¢

THIS IS THE MASS
By Henri Daniel-Rops. Photographs of Bishop Fulton J. Sheen
by Karsh   D90—95¢

THE ORIGIN OF THE JESUITS
By James Brodrick, S.J.
                       D91—85¢

**A POPULAR HISTORY OF THE
REFORMATION**
By Philip Hughes   D92—95¢

THE RESTLESS FLAME
By Louis de Wohl   D93—85¢

PROGRESS AND RELIGION
By Christopher Dawson
                       D94—85¢

**THE CATHOLIC CHURCH IN THE
MODERN WORLD**
By E. E. Y. Hales   D95—95¢

THE LIFE OF TERESA OF JESUS:
The Autobiography of St. Teresa of Avila. Translated and
with an introduction by E. Allison Peers   D96—$1.25

GIANTS OF THE FAITH
By John A. O'Brien   D97—95¢

SCHOLASTICISM AND POLITICS
By Jacques Maritain   D98—95¢

THE SON OF GOD
By Karl Adam   D99—85¢

THE MAN WHO WAS CHESTERTON
Edited by Raymond T. Bond
                       D100—$1.45

IMAGE BOOKS

Image Books constitute a quality library of Catholic writings, broad in human interest and deep in Christian insight. They will include classical Christian writings, devotion, philosophy, education and history; biographies, novels and poetry; and books on contemporary social problems. They represent a planned program of making available to the widest possible audience the finest Catholic literature in attractive, paper-bound, inexpensive editions. They have been selected with these criteria in mind: that they must in every instance be well written, inspiring to the spirit, and of lasting value to the general audience who will purchase them.

The majority of Image Books will consist of reprints made possible through the cooperation of the publishers of the original editions. Occasionally certain much-needed volumes which are not available will also be initiated for this series.

A descriptive catalogue of the Image Books already published may be obtained by writing directly to the publisher. Comments and suggestions from those interested in the series are welcomed by the publisher.   3